Treason From Within

A True Story of a Marriage

Gayle Frances Larkin

This is a true story although some of the names have been altered to protect those who are still alive.

ISBN 978-1-7398505-2-4

A nation can survive its fools, and even the ambitious. But it cannot survive treason from within. An enemy at the gates is less formidable, for he is known and carries his banner openly. But the traitor moves amongst those within the gates freely, his sly whispers rustling through the alleys, heard in the very halls of government itself.

Marcus Tullius Cicero

Author's Note

We are living in a time where the explosion of news has uncovered some serious shortcomings in our laws to protect wives and children. This tale shows some of the tricky predicaments that befell one mother and her efforts to resolve each one as it unfolded. No doubt you may vociferously disagree with some of her reasoning, and her proffered solutions.

Here you will be able to see how the wife kept herself free from some of the worst traps laid for her, and how she was able to find her 'teaspoon of hope'.

This story is based on events that happened in real life which unfolded much as told with the proviso that anyone concerned who is still alive has not been included, with the exception of the mother, the daughter and one other person who has given permission to be included. I have tried to corroborate every incident. Where the person concerned denied any memory of that event, I have excluded it. This is an abbreviated account, which, I hope, will help you to avoid the mistakes that caused my lack of understanding.

If possible, I hope you can find some humour, and some enjoyment in this book.

Gayle Frances Larkin

Contents

Prologue

The winter sun was shining bright and warm on the single storey homes and the head height brick walls with security gates surrounding tiny gardens. No cars were on the street. Nobody was anywhere to be seen. The silence was almost tangible. A grey slate roof topped the palest yellow paint on the brick walls of the substantial house. Light pink jasmine blooms with the hot pink bougainvillea and buddleia flowers mingled their perfumes in the still afternoon. Peace seemed to be encased in the little front garden. The immediate shrill of the doorbell was different as the petite woman ran to answer its urgent summons.

At the locked gate in the high wall two policemen waited, idly scanning the property.

'We would like to speak to your husband about a murder,' said one of the dark blue uniforms through the gate when he saw the tiny woman standing behind the second black iron gate that prevented entry to the house.

Stunned, Ellen Phipps thought: *So, he was involved in the death,* but answered: 'He's at the university.'

'No, he isn't,' the other blue uniform answered.

'Then I don't know where he is. He's supposed to be lecturing to students,' she said, mentioning the local university.

The two men left after mentioning the usual request to let her husband know they wanted to interview him.

Alone, she sat motionless, unable to think or to realise the magnitude of the charge that now violated her world.

Chapter 1

Ellen was born into a fiery family. Her father was the son of a Norwegian and Irish Roman Catholic mother who was said to have 'the second sight', and an Episcopalian father whose family emigrated from Germany to America, and who demanded absolute obedience of any child. After a family argument, her very good looking grandfather joined the Yorkshire Rifles and was sent to Johannesburg to recuperate. He met this mercurial woman who could be an entrancing mimic and married her. The only son of this marriage was said to look like Ronald Colman, a film star who was very popular during the 1940's and 1950's, was a casualty of the second World War who never allowed any discussion on wars, religion, sex, or politics.

Ellen's father worked in the mines as a statistician. His mathematical abilities were constantly the amazement of any who knew him. Later, he visited the dream hotel of an accountant who had personally supervised, and brought to completion, what was familiarly known as 'Sin City' as it had casinos, and tried to fulfil any of the most extravagant wishes. It was situated in a neighbouring country, just outside the borders of South Africa. Her father would sit and watch the gambling for about twenty minutes then he would join in the session. It was not long before the security guard tapped him on the shoulder and requested his company. Intrigued, he followed. He was led to a security room where, it was said, over two hundred cameras monitored the proceedings. Politely he was asked to take a seat. They wanted to know the secret of his winnings.

'You start watching the game, look at the angle of the table, then apply a fifty four percent chance of winning then -,' by this time no one hearing him could understand his concept. When he tried for the third time to explain his thought processes he was told: 'Thank you for your explanation. I don't understand it. But, please, don't come back again, we can't afford to have people like you here. We'd go out of business.' He laughed, and shook hands with the men present, and did not return to that massive construction.

Ellen's blonde mother was proud she was the only sibling to have graduated from a university. Her degree majoring in English and Geography would have enabled her to teach at a school, but she refused to study for the required diploma. As soon as she had passed the final examinations for her degree, her parents took her on a holiday in Messina (now Musina) near the Limpopo River and the border of Southern Rhodesia which today is known as Zimbabwe. Here she met a captain who had been in the army but who was later employed in the strategic industry that was mining. Without a second thought, she wrote to her fiancé, and broke off their engagement of two years. She had not even heard the captain speak one word. Ellen's grandfather was furious, anxious, and upset that his daughter would marry a man 'of the world'. The grandfather was a retired Free Mason who was a strict teetotal with a terror of the heavy drinking Roman Catholic war veteran. The fiancé whose own father was a judge, later himself became a judge, and so was a 'man of a respectable family'.

Her lay minister grandfather had caught her cheating in a game of cards with him when she was only four years old. He considered she 'was consorting with the devil', and refused to play with her ever again, something she always remembered. As a child born so long after her two brothers, who were pilots in the Royal Air Force fighting for the Allies, and virtually ignored by her father, she was used to getting her own way. She was competitive beyond any reasonable limit, and would sulk or throw a tantrum to achieve her end. She married her captain, and they settled into life in Johannesburg.

When Ellen was about three months old there was a row, shouting by Mrs Phipps and her mother in law. This was just before midnight. Hearing the ruckus Ellen's nanny ran swiftly to the main room of the house just in time to see Mrs Phipps grab the baby from her mother in law's arms and hurl her towards the brick wall. The nanny sprinted to catch Ellen before her head could hit the brick wall.

On a lovely sunny morning, the baby in her pram was wheeled out onto the verandah. Biscuit, a wire-haired fox terrier, regarded the baby as her prize possession, to be guarded against any danger. At first the morning was quiet. Suddenly the growling became barking, then Biscuit rushed at the pram and grabbed the cobra by the throat as it lifted itself off the floor to attack Ellen. They twisted around and around on the floor with the snake striking Biscuit repeatedly in the neck, but Biscuit held onto her prey; severing its head from its body. A little while later, Biscuit died in the arms of Mr Phipps who shed tears at the tragedy that befell his beloved pet when saving Ellen's life.

Ellen's mother liked to call herself a Methodist, and she enjoyed telling her six year old daughter about a book purporting to tell the most horrific stories about Roman Catholic practices. This terrified the child. The book was later proved to have been published to make money out of a non-existent scandal: the narrator was delusional. But this was never told to the child who was then preparing for her reception of the sacraments. Her father no longer attended any services at the local church. The priest, who was a Roman Catholic convert, told Ellen that she would not be given any absolution for her sins unless she brought her father 'back into the fold'. Ellen was terrified. Her father rushed to the priest's home to 'knock some sense into the man'. To his frustration, the priest was away from his home.

Ellen, was sent to different schools as the family moved from the Transvaal (now Gauteng) to Natal (now Kwa-Zulu Natal), then back to Johannesburg. Each province had different subjects at schools, for example, one had botany another had biology; they also vied with each other, each proclaiming it had the higher standards of education in the country.

Her schools ranged from convents for girls only to state co-educational ones. She tumbled from one to the other across provincial lines with different subjects. She started school on the day of an examination never having studied the course, or she may upset the class by achieving the top marks in the English one. The social circles had already been formed when she started at each new school, and the girls showed clearly, they did not want any newcomers. She kept herself occupied with Red Cross courses and examinations (where available), or combed the school libraries for books she devoured.

Her American great-uncle had written to her aunt saying he did not want any of his family in South Africa to grow up like barbarians so he gave her some money with the express order to purchase some books by Charles Dickens, the greatest writer ever, or so he thought. It was a week before her eighth birthday when Ellen was given a copy of *Great Expectations*. She walked to the convent on the side of the road reading the book. She carried on reading it on her way home, and when she finished the book, she started it all over again. She was set alight: she identified so closely with Pip who had been 'brought up by hand', just as she had been. She devoured *Oliver Twist,* then *A Christmas Carol.* From now on, the great love of her life was Charles Dickens. When she was sixteen, she became the youngest member of the local branch of the Dickens Fellowship. This branch was soon dissolved, but her pursuit of this author's books, or any about him, continued throughout her life.

The young Ellen remembered the big family gatherings around the Christmas tree in the corner of the lounge at her grandfather's house in Durban. Mornings were spent on the beach where the children became roasted red lobsters on their arrival at lunch time. Some of the family members used to watch the horses prancing around the paddock at the back of the house. Once the nine year old Ellen was standing, too terrified to move, holding tightly to the top rail of the paddock while her seventy five year old grandfather rushed into the paddock, and pulled the jockey away from a maddened stallion. He walked slowly but purposefully up to the wild animal, grabbed the bridle all the while talking quietly and calmly looking into its eyes. Mrs Phipps kept repeating: 'Oh, my God! He's going to be killed!' Ellen, beside her, said not a word, her eyes glued to the situation before her. In a very short space of time her grandfather leapt up onto the horse and led it round and round the paddock in ever smaller circles until the stallion knew his master and obeyed him implicitly. It was a master class in how to break a spirited stallion without a whip, without anger, using only strength of character and kindness. Later he threatened to have the jockey barred if he ever mistreated a horse again.

Mrs Phipps ignored her eleven year old daughter and did not speak to her for six months even though they were living in the same house.

Soon after the twelve year old Ellen reached Johannesburg and started at yet another school, the school inspector arrived for his assessment of it. The English lesson had just begun. He politely asked the class to write one paragraph on any subject. Ellen chose to write a passage that she had imagined. It was about eight steps to the front glass doors of her block of flats. A girl in a wheelchair arrived and was uncertain how she could enter the building. The two of them smiled at each other. The writer thought it was 'uncanny' how she knew what the girl was thinking. She ran down the steps and showed her the way to the car entrance which was just yards away. The inspector was excited about such a young child using the word 'uncanny'. He persuaded her headmistress to arrange a bursary for the girl eventually to attend university. Which she did.

When her mother and father were told of the bursary and the relevant conditions attached to it, they called this 'charity', then refused to allow it to be given to Ellen. They then arranged for Ellen to attend accounting classes instead of her beloved English ones. Ellen was heartbroken. She said she would rather die. She was told to stop being so childish. They never knew how true Ellen's statement was. Her disrupted schooling meant she had lost vital years in arithmetic and mathematics classes, years never to be recovered. Accounting and taxation classes held innumerable terrors for her. She learnt to overcome these by learning the rules, laws, and calculations by rote until she eventually understood the rationale behind those subjects.

At fifteen she had to walk to the college through what was popularly known as 'murder mile', and then had to return home using the same route. She finished her schooling and began to work in accounting while attending night lectures until 8.15 p.m.

One night she was given a fright when a big, burly man accosted her.

'What are your parents doing, allowing a little girl like you to roam around at night?'

'It's the only way home after my lectures,' was all she could think to answer.

'Don't worry, I'll see you home. I'm in the orchestra.' Ellen now saw the violin he was carrying. He went on to tell her he was Russian, and proud of it. She thought his command of the English language was amazing. They chatted until she reached the block of flats where she was living with her family. She never saw him again. This was one of the many times she would learn that a stranger could be kinder to her than any member of her own family.

She heard someone say the Holocaust was not true. Her father and her two uncles had fought in World War II on the side of the Allies. Were these people saying this war was all for nothing? Why then were so many nations united in their determination to defeat the Axis powers? She decided to investigate, and walked into the main Johannesburg Central Library. She wound her way until she reached the reference section where the books telling the stories of the World Wars were kept. She found the first volume on the Nuremberg Trials. She took it down from the shelf and went to sit in one of the leather seats near a small round table. Tucked away behind the tall shelving unit she opened the book and started to read. She recognised very few of the names but she looked at the index and then started at the beginning of the introduction. After a very long time she realised the care, time and wealth of knowledge that was embroiled in those processes. There were so many photographs of the appalling atrocities. She quickly stopped looking at these desecrations of human life. She believed so wholeheartedly in the abomination of fascism. She now determined to argue against it whenever it arose in her discussions. This led to some very spirited arguments among her peers.

Once she borrowed a book of Aristotle's letters and was reading his views of what he called ill-mannered behaviour out loud to her mother. She could not believe how people could hold similar views even when they were thousands of years apart, as well as being from such different cultures.

After a few years she was still working in the hated field of figures. She was a natural with languages, but she could be deceived easily when dealing with numbers. She learnt different ways of ensuring that all the amounts agreed to zero. Any discrepancy would be immediately highlighted. This saved her hours in balancing her books.

In this manner Ellen supported her family for more than seven years when she decided to talk to her mother about her dreams for her future. For years she had been forced to swim in the shark infested waters of accountancy, now she tried to escape.

'Would I be able to attend the university when it starts the new year in January?'

'Why? Surely you have a good job at a very reasonable salary. Anyway, you're too old now.'

'I have a letter of acceptance as a mature student, and I've saved enough to pay for the first term.'

'Your father will have a lot to say. You know we rely on you to keep the family going.'

'When is it my turn to have a degree? You did…'

'Don't be silly! That's different! I had scholarships…'

'You told Daddy to refuse the one I was offered by the headmistress of my school.'

'You're being ridiculous now,' her mother closed the conversation.

Eventually, they agreed she could attend the university. After the second week she was told, she would have to work in her father's employer's offices to help pay her way. She was allowed precisely one hour for her lecture and her father would be waiting outside the main gate to fetch her.

It was in the third month her mother demanded she hand over all her savings.

'That money belongs to the university…'

'We will pay it for you later. We need it now.'

When she received the second letter of demand for payment of her fees, she approached her mother.

'Will you pay this account now? It's very late.'

'You'll have to pay it yourself. You know we have no money.'

'You took everything I had.'

'All right, then! I'll pay it, but you'll have to pay me back!'

Ellen realised she would never be allowed to live her own life so she went back to work. At the end of the first month of her employment she asked her employer for a loan of nearly a third of her monthly salary. She told him she wanted to leave home and to live in a furnished apartment. He agreed.

On 1st April she moved out of the house with a box of her few books, her study notes, and her clothing. Was the date prophetic?

She met Father Victor, a Franciscan priest who was the dean of studies of the local seminary for the formation of Roman Catholic priests.

She had been introduced to him at an evening Mass for university students. This was held in Pretoria. Everyone later adjourned to a hall, where there was a vigorous debate, as if there could be anything else when students were having fun. Father Victor celebrated the Mass in the traditional garments, and then presided over the evening dressed in his Franciscan habit with the usual sandals which are an important part of the uniform. Ellen felt she had received a psychic shock: there was such a sense of familiarity and an almost casual air about everything, whereas previously she had been to formal Masses.

Father Victor talked about how 'Abba' was used almost like 'Daddy', a familiar greeting, and not a more distanced, artificial one. There was no question that Father Victor was anything but wholly engrossed in his religious life: it superseded every other interest for him. His genuine warmth, humility, and complete interest in those he addressed was something Ellen had never before experienced. She was forever changed by this evening, and was later to work with him on different projects.

She had reached the age of twenty two, and had supported her siblings through school. She wrote a letter to Father Victor asking where she could best use her skills. She was working for an accounting and auditing firm, and had also attended night lectures that allowed her to sit for the international examinations in English, statistics, economics, company law, taxation, and other subjects.

The letter was shown to her mother who had a pathological hatred of the Roman Catholic religion. Mrs Phipps was terrified that her eldest child would leave the home and she would lose the control of Ellen's salary.

Chapter 2

The family found a student who seemed to meander through his life. They engineered the meetings between Ellen and the student, ensuring she would be frequently in the company of the student and her family. Zack Farthing was about six feet in height, with fair hair, and he had the typical shoulders of a rugby player. He wore thick, black rimmed spectacles so it was not immediately obvious that he could see out of one eye only, and his vision in that eye was less than twenty five per cent. To compensate he used to lean his head slightly to one side. He wanted, above all else, to be pitied. His eyes were the perfect excuse: then everyone would allow him exceptional leniency to be able to do exactly what he wanted. He appeared warm and charming, eager to please, all the while decrying his disability. He was about twenty months younger than Ellen, of the same religion, and Mrs Phipps was positive that he would grow bored with her daughter very quickly.

At the main Sunday morning Mass, Zack managed to try to sit in front of Ellen so she would be impressed with his piety. He quickly realised that she was isolated within the family unit and used his facile charm to try to engage with her. He would discuss economics, law, and politics with her when they met, always careful to defer to her. He knew this was not the treatment accorded her by her family members.

Zack's fight with life began the moment he was born. An instrument baby, he had had his first eye operation in England when he was six months old. Ellen was told his mother was too traumatised to deal properly with her baby so her sister came often to help with his care, especially in his first year. This aunt adored him and to her he could do no wrong. The aunt had lost her own son soon after his birth due to hospital neglect. Her adored husband was an extreme casualty of the war so she was unable to have any further children. Her love was lavished on her husband as well as on her disabled nephew.

He was sent to a school for boys only where he stayed until he matriculated. As a big child he was proud of bullying the smaller ones. His parents were called to a conference when he was in Standard 5 (Year 7) and warned that at the next infraction of their rules he would be expelled. He began to behave properly. In later years he was proud of this incident. Was this the time that he learnt that public image is paramount, and everything and every one else is to be sacrificed to that magnificent public image?

He always laughed at the memory of how he had tried to attack a family member with a heavily oiled cricket bat when he was fifteen. Later, when she knew more about Zack, Ellen wondered if this story was true, but she would never know. Another memory in which he delighted was the idea that his two grandfathers fought on opposite sides in World War II, and he would dwell on the idea of the two men trying to shoot at each other. Ellen was horrified at the idea of anyone enjoying this horror. But, was this true?

He was said to have played rugby at school, and excelled at bowling in cricket, and always enjoyed discussing any sporting activities.

In his matriculation year, he was sent to be evaluated by the National Institute. They wrote that his ability with mathematics was excellent, and that he could be a physicist, while his ability with language was just average.

Then his mother died when he was seventeen.

After he matriculated, he was sent to Europe on a six week package tour. This tour remained in his mind for many years

The South African government used conscription as a means of training for military service. At the beginning of the first year after his schooling had finished, he decided to go to the relevant government office with the various boys from his school who had been called up to complete the obligatory two years. Zack sat and listened as the boys read out aloud from the chart to check their eyesight. He memorised the list. When his turn came to be medically examined, they started with the eye check. The doctor, without appearing to do so, looked at the incredibly thick lenses of the subject of his latest examination. He was suspicious. Zack 'read' the chart perfectly.

'Good. Now read the number plate of the car across the road.'

Zack peered, then admitted: 'What car? I can't see one.'

'Yes, it's a VW. You know, you would have been a liability. You could have been in a position to kill one of your own men in a war situation. Why did you do this?' The doctor had not been fooled for a minute.

Zack did not pretend to misunderstand: 'Because I wanted to go with my class. They're all going to Welkom.'

Zack began his articles with a firm of accountants and auditors when he first started studying at university. He later abandoned his articles after eighteen months. He continued studying for his Bachelor of Commerce degree. He wanted to go into criminal law, he said. That meant he would have to study for a postgraduate degree, and attend evening classes at the university while working at a law firm during the day. But at that time, he was working at casual administrative jobs, and at a liquor store on Saturday mornings in between his daytime classes. Then he met Ellen.

He told her he wanted her to teach him good manners as he had never learnt how to behave correctly in polite society. He did not tell her that he had absolutely no time for this type of behaviour. He simply was being sycophantic. He wanted to take her to an intellectual talk at the university but did not know how to arrange his transport. While he was showing her the difficulties he was experiencing because he could not drive a vehicle to enlist greater sympathy for him, he was also hinting at their shared intellectual interests. He asked her to join him for a cup of coffee.

One morning Zack managed to be included in a student protest against the government. He was in the front line of the gathering. They were extremely agitated, and believed that their intransigence would force their will on the recalcitrant government, at least that was the prevailing view of those students Ellen met. Some of those protesting students were jailed. She did not realise how Zack was keeping her away from his family members, and usual companions. This was the beginning of the isolation Zack went to great trouble to enforce.

Her parents tried the ignoring, silent treatment with Ellen again. Zack saw this as a great opportunity to show understanding and support for her home situation. She continued to go to work and, in her turn, disregarded the manner and scope of the treatment she received.

The great upheaval was caused when her parents decided that Ellen would not be allowed to leave her home except to go to work. She was not allowed to see anyone. She was not allowed to learn to drive a motor vehicle.

Driven to distraction by the demands imposed upon her, Ellen moved into her furnished flat which had a telephone connected to an exchange system at the reception desk. Ellen was happy that she would be safe and able to be in immediate contact with the outside world if any difficulty arose. She liked her one bedroom apartment with its own combined lounge and dining room, separate kitchen, and full bathroom. She easy access to the bus system, and would have no difficulties with transport.

Chapter 3

Just over two months later Ellen's life was to be changed dramatically.

The winter's night was dark, clear, and cool but brightly lit by the surrounding buildings and the Cathedral as the congregation spilled out over the pavements, roads and into cars or walked home.

Ellen and Zack were walking towards the steep hill they would have to climb to arrive at her flat.

'Why can't we get engaged?' Zack pressed.

'I've not thought of marriage at this time,' Ellen replied quietly, astounded. 'I was thinking of going to university to read English, Philosophy and Biblical Studies.'

'Well, think of it now. You can always go to university after I have finished my studies. You know I would have married you anyhow. Why not get married in August?'

'You can't have thought this through. How can you come up with a wedding in a mere six weeks? And you do know what everyone will think, don't you?'

'Look, my final examinations are in October. If the wedding is in August it doesn't interfere with them. Not the 17th because that's the anniversary of the day my mother died.'

'We're not even engaged.'

'We could get engaged the week before that. What about my mother's birthday, the 5th?'

'I'm not so very sure about that. There's a very real possibility I cannot have children. It's too big an imposition to place on a man – to deprive him of heirs. This is completely out of the blue.'

Zack was in his own world when she had stopped speaking.

'That's fine. I won't have to share you with anyone. You can concentrate on me, can't you?' Zack said quickly.

The following week Zack met Ellen for a cup of coffee. He mentioned the possibility of him going blind.

'We can deal with that, if it happens. I read in the newspaper of an American couple where the husband went blind after qualifying as an attorney. He was a trial lawyer who appeared in court, and he married a woman who read everything to him out loud. She also qualified as an attorney so now he is able to conduct his trials while she researches the law, the cases, and reads everything to him. They are an inspiring couple. We can do the same. I'll read English when you've finished the LLB. It will be a wonderful start for us as a team.'

Zack did not reply to this suggestion, but quickly dropped the subject, and started to talk about the final arrangements for the wedding.

Zack knew that his university studies were no longer being funded. A colleague had jokingly mentioned that he would not mind marrying Ellen as she earned a good salary, enough to be able to live comfortably, and also to fund his law studies. She was reasonable looking, and she could cook. Within forty eight hours Zack was certain he had won the battle with his colleague. He overlooked the fact his colleague had never spoken to Ellen, and also that the man's family was wealthy, so he would have no need of any wife to fund him. He was enjoying taunting Zack in the rivalry that was endemic to these students. Zack did not mention that she would have to pay for his fees and support him financially. It never occurred to him to apply for a bank loan. As he reasoned, his wife was now responsible for his tertiary education.

Ellen was surprised when one student was shocked at the engagement, hinting she had prior entitlement. Ellen was blunt: the only people involved were the family members. Zack then escorted Ellen off the campus so he could freely 'explain' his engagement without the encumbrance of Ellen's presence. This was the first time Ellen experienced a chill at his behaviour. Since he was so concerned for a stranger, and not for his prospective wife, what did this portend for her future life?

The day was quiet, especially for a university campus. The students were not around, standing in groups chatting, or walking to the various buildings. Ellen had left work and arrived at the law school offices to meet Zack as arranged. As she walked past an open door, she was rugby tackled to the ground by a law student.

'Are you mad? Don't you know better than to be here?'

'I'm meeting my fiancé.'

'He should have warned you not to be on the campus. There are bullets flying everywhere, you could be killed.'

They waited for half an hour then checked to see that there were no policemen around before Ellen made her way to her destination. Zack was completely oblivious of anything but his own interests. According to Zack, the student did not know what he was talking about. She was safe, wasn't she? He, Zack, was engaged in proper confrontations to help society. Ellen did not tell him important people with appropriate support and connections could effect lasting change. Surely, he was supposed to be involved with his studies only; he was conflating politics and education. They were two separate entities.

It was obligatory for the engaged couple to attend instruction classes to help to equip them for their future life. These classes were gladly undertaken by Father Victor in Pretoria. He gently tried to show that real life is not the same as the one envisaged, and each one was to be a support to the other. He covered all the religious themes: did they welcome children? Zack was enthusiastic in his agreement, which sat oddly with his idea of wanting Ellen to be solely concentrated on him alone. The evenings were so inclusive that Ellen began to feel really enthusiastic about her future life.

One evening Ellen's mother suggested she go to the family home for supper, her mother would fetch her from a pre-arranged place in the centre of Johannesburg. Ellen agreed. Afterwards, her parents sat with her in front of a magnificent gas fire that kept the house cosy. Her mother was quiet so her father started: 'You know, you don't have to get married. You can live here very comfortably even your laundry would be done for you.' Ellen realised the sub-text: her mother wanted her back under their control, and with her salary to enable them to afford any luxuries her mother might want. She realised the moment was tricky.

'It's all arranged. We have already completed the pre-marriage course.'

A few days before the wedding Zack had arranged to meet Ellen. Just before she went to get ready to meet him, he telephoned her and told her he would not be seeing her as he had been asked to escort a woman to a function for her twenty first birthday celebration. He knew her brother. Their family had all the appearances of wealth.

'But you're engaged: we're getting married on the twelfth!'

'So, what? That doesn't change anything.'

'Have you hired a proper suit?'

'No, I'll wear my ordinary grey suit.'

'That will be an insult to her and to her family.'

Ellen looked up the telephone number in the directory and asked to speak to the birthday girl. After wishing her a happy birthday Ellen was asked who she was: she replied that she was Zack's fiancée, and when asked about the wedding she told her it was on the twelfth of August.

This incident made Ellen wonder if the wedding would actually take place. Her trust was being eroded further in Zack.

In his next surprise to everyone, Zack decided to have an ante-nuptial agreement drawn up. He was adamant that as a criminal lawyer his family home would be at risk, and he wanted to protect it. This was done and signed. Zack did not tell Ellen that if the goods conferred in the agreement were not given to her within five years, she would have no entitlement to them. This was the first critical lie, although it was not known for many years.

Ellen did not like any of the current fashions for her wedding dress so she designed it herself. She found a pattern that could be adapted and felt it would be adequate, especially with the guipure lace used as an accent.

Chapter 4

Rain fell for most of the day of the wedding. Ellen had an early appointment with her hairdresser in town. She had asked her mother to fetch her so she would not be drenched on the way to the family home out in the northern suburbs. Besides, the infrequent buses took so long to arrive, and even longer to reach their destination. Mrs Phipps flatly refused, and added: 'You must be quick. You have to wash the chandelier when you arrive here.'

When she eventually arrived at her mother's house, she rang the doorbell. She reached a bedroom, put all the paraphernalia she had carried with her down, then rushed to the bathroom to prepare for her wedding. Within minutes Mrs Phipps was hammering on the bathroom door: 'You don't have time for a bath! You still have to wash the chandelier!' Ellen ignored her. She repaired the damage the rain had caused to her hairdo, and quickly slipped into her wedding gown.

After the ceremony, the sun crept out and shone weakly. There were very few guests at the reception as Ellen's family had had six immediate family members buried in the weeks between the engagement and the wedding day. These included Ellen's maternal grandmother, her eldest son, and his eldest daughter's husband, all in the same hospital over the same weekend. Not one of them knew that the other family members were also dying then.

Zack left Ellen on her own throughout the entire reception. She decided to enjoy chatting to the members of her extended family now that the rush was over.

Zack and Ellen arrived at the hotel and were shown to their room. He stood at the window looking at the traffic below, his hands in his pockets, silent. Ellen asked him, a regular teapot, if he would like a cup of tea to drink. He swung round and muttered under his breath, words that Ellen's sharp ears heard. She understood then there was no sacrament of marriage in his eyes, whatever he may have said to the contrary. She knew any trust in him was now extinguished. This was no basis for a marriage. There was nothing she could do – no one she could ask for help. But real life did not allow anything but its own trajectory. She was hurried along a path trodden by countless women before. Only she herself could determine her own destiny: she would have to be principled, and strong.

On Monday morning early the bridal couple caught the bus into town. After a quick breakfast at a café, they went their separate ways: Ellen to work while Zack left her at the door of the building where her office was located.

That evening after she started cooking the evening meal, Zack took a telephone call which lasted more than two hours. When asked about it, he said it was confidential. She asked him where his loyalties lay? She was entitled to his as she was his wife. Zack ignored this interjection: her comments were irrelevant. The supper was almost inedible. After this exchange it was inevitable the evening would end in a row. Zack felt entitled, and Ellen was bitterly hurt.

The second evening was almost a repetition, except this time Ellen put what she had cooked into the bin. The third evening she did not cook at all. Zack was furious.

'If you're not ready to eat, it is pointless cooking anything,' was the only reply Ellen gave.

The fourth night there was no telephone call – Ellen cooked while Zack leant against a wall, telling her about his day.

Three weeks after the wedding Ellen noticed Zack had acquired a habit of staring unblinkingly at a wall, the muscles were petrified in his green-white face. He seemed unable to hear or to be reached by any outside stimulus. This terrified Ellen. She called it his 'fugue'.

After work the next evening she contacted her parish priest for help in her terror at her new husband's behaviour, only to be told: 'You're bored, and trying to evade your responsibility'. Ellen realised one really lives only in one's own mind. She decided to keep herself occupied so she did what she learnt to do at all the different schools she had attended: read, and keep on reading. Then she would not have time to be distracted or bored.

A week later they moved into an unfurnished flat without a telephone. They were also in a new parish. Ellen was relieved. Now she thought they would be able to build their relationship into a secure family unit. They had furnished the flat very simply. Ellen had entered into a hire purchase agreement with a mid-range firm of furniture suppliers where she purchased lined curtains, and lace curtains for the sitting room and the bedroom, a sofa with two matching chairs, a bed, and a refrigerator with a top freezer section. The following week they chose a dining room table with four chairs. Later they would be able to add to these basics.

With no distractions to entertain them, Zack studied for his examinations while Ellen cooked, and coped with the household chores after she had finished work for the day. He discussed a few of the concepts he was studying with Ellen as she had already passed those examinations in the same subjects.

Three months later there were tears in Ellen's father in law's eyes as he said to her:

'I thought you'd destroyed my son's life by marrying him, but he's passed the finals for his degree! You've made him!'

'There was nothing else for him to do. Only studying,' Ellen replied, embarrassed.

Zack signed a contract to be articled to a principal in a well-known firm of attorneys. During the term time any student was allowed to leave work early to attend the evening lectures that were being held at the university. He gave the impression of relishing the work as well as the usual socialising that happened after the day had ended. He sternly told Ellen she was not welcome at these events, and he would not tell her where they were held. She knew trouble was brewing, but did not know how to prevent it. She tried to reason with him but he refused to discuss it.

He shared an office with another clerk who was wealthy and rude. Jonah disliked women, not bothering to greet them when they arrived to join the group where he remained, slouched in his chair. His hair looked as though it had never met a comb. His background allowed him to join in many exciting and dangerous activities. Zack revelled in Jonah's rudeness, disrespect for authority, and complete callousness.

He and Ellen were invited to spend a long weekend in a neighbouring town with this family. Zack was eager to go, but Ellen said they did not live at the same level so would not be able to reciprocate.

Zack was of the opinion that this did not matter. This was the cause of the greatest row between Zack and Ellen.

Ellen started having a dream about green curtains that completely covered one wall which was only windows from the ceiling to the floor. There were no voile or lace curtains at the windows, and the dark wooden floor was uncovered. Chairs were placed around the walls of the empty room which looked out onto a green lawn.

In another place there was a massive fire then suddenly she and Zack were at the railway station trying to book tickets unsuccessfully to a far destination.

Each night the dream returned with greater clarity, depth, and urgency. She was frantic to save the life that was needlessly lost. This went on for five nights, each day as she returned to work her colleague would ask: 'Did you have the dream last night?'

The answer was always the same: 'Yes'.

On Saturday morning they tried to book train tickets to the town where his colleague had lived: Jonah had been burned to death in a glider. No tickets were available.

Monday afternoon Zack came home early to say they would be travelling in the car with his principal to attend the funeral. The whole firm would be going in a convoy of motor vehicles as a mark of respect.

The next time Ellen saw her colleague, Ellen was told that she never wanted to hear of any dream ever again. The bereaved family had a room with long green curtains, just as Ellen had seen in her dreams.

Every November Zack would head up the memorial list for the Masses for the Dead with the name of this colleague. One year it was the only name.

Zack's first case as an attorney was to defend a man who was accused of a capital offense. This meant the death penalty was a major factor in the defence of the accused who had openly acknowledged his guilt of the crime. Zack spent hours working on the case but was unable to bring in a verdict that would have saved the man's life. The direct result of this event was that Zack applied to be a lecturer at the school of law at the local university. He was not accepted. A year later he was accepted when he applied for the second time.

Chapter 5

Each Saturday evening, they went to Mass. Soon their faces were familiar, if unknown. The parish was a peripatetic one, with a migrant turnover every three months, as well as having a few of the old established families. The parish priest, Father Thomas, a Jesuit priest, decided to lock the front doors to the church, leaving only the side doors open. Then he stood at the foot of the stairs, greeting each person as they were leaving the church building. Zack introduced himself and Ellen. Then he invited the priest to an evening meal after his examinations. This was graciously accepted. The two men continued discussing the play, *A Man for All Seasons.* Zack generously offered his copy of the book to be read, saying that Ellen would bring it to the presbytery.

A month later Ellen was asked to help with the arrangement of the church flowers for the weekend services. She agreed. Each Saturday afternoon Ellen was to be found in the cold room adjoining the sanctuary. Zack was engaged with his university work, whatever that was.

It was not long before Father Thomas was arriving for a light supper on Sunday evenings. The three of them would sit and discuss the topics of the day.

A few weeks later, one of the wealthier parishioners tackled Ellen:

'Don't you know you shouldn't monopolise Father Thomas every Sunday evening?'

'He has almost no groceries in his kitchen. Aren't we supposed to look after our parish priests? Why don't you ask him for a meal? He would love that,' Ellen replied.

Two weeks later the woman arrived at the presbytery with a platter filled with cooked lobster, crayfish, and other succulent dishes for the Good Friday meals.

Father Thomas grumbled: 'She's very kind. We can't refuse, but she has entirely prevented the penitential spirit of Good Friday!'

The parishioners were warm hearted and often asked their priest to a meal, and sometimes to a day spent in the warm sunshine with their families after the Sunday services.

When he drove home after a hospital visit, Father Thomas would arrive at Ellen's front door, knock on it, and call out: 'Tea time!' Or sometimes he would telephone Ellen. When she answered, he would order: 'Put the kettle on,' without any other greeting, and replace the receiver.

Over cups of tea, he and Ellen would discuss everything, even the joke of St Theresa of Avila and St John of the Cross. The two saints had been travelling in Spain, and had arrived at the inn to discover that chicken casserole, St Theresa's favourite dish, was prepared. She had been to confession so St John said: 'Theresa, remember penance'. To which she replied: 'Ah, when penance, penance, but when chicken, chicken!'

One time Father Thomas told her: 'You're so lucky to have so much land in South Africa.' Ellen replied: 'There's a lot of land in England, too. It's just in too few hands. We live in houses on one eighth of an acre, so why does one man think he's entitled to have an extra 249,000 acres?'

Their discussions ranged over books, poetry, music, and many other topics.

Six months later Father Thomas would bring the Sunday collections to their flat. After they had enjoyed the supper Ellen had cooked, the three of them would sit around the dining room table and count the different coins and bag them according to their denominations. This activity saved Father Thomas hours of his time. Eventually Ellen would spend the whole of Easter Monday counting the collections, and getting it ready to be banked.

At night Father Thomas was often called out to the hospital for patients who were dying. Afterwards he would travel along the road, and would look at the block of flats which he passed on his way home. Everything was in darkness. If he saw a light on, he would stop his car and go speedily and quietly up to the door and give his usual greeting, a knock on the door while simultaneously calling out softly: 'Tea time!'

Ellen would open the door, and allow him to precede her. His greeting to Zack would be rough and demanding: 'Why haven't you put the kettle on? We're having tea.' Usually this was sufficient to bring Zack out of his 'fugue', and he would obediently rise from his armchair, and go silently into the kitchen. The sounds of the kettle being filled with water, and the cups and saucers being rattled against the kitchen counter helped to defuse the tension.

'How long has he been like this, this time?'

'Roughly four hours.'

'We'll talk later.'

'Where have you been, at the hospital again?'

'Yes. A shooting.'

'Is the person all right?'

'No. He died.'

When Zack entered the room with the tea already made in the cups, he started a normal conversation with Father Thomas. The green-white colour of his face had returned to its normal state, while the muscles were no longer set, and petrified. When the tea cups were empty, Father Thomas stood up and told them they should be asleep at that time. His quiet presence often defused the violence in Zack and kept this family safe, as he did for so many other families. He saw the physical welfare of his parishioners as part of his pastoral care as well as his other priestly duties. He was the only person outside the little family who had seen these episodes when they occurred.

It was not long before he brought his brother, Father Richard, who was also a Jesuit priest, to visit their home. The kitchen light was not working so Father Richard asked for a ladder and a towel to be brought to him. On top of the ladder, he suddenly demanded a hammer be given to him. Then he smashed the light, and gleefully said: 'That's fixed it!'

Everyone burst out laughing.

Two years later Ellen was still finding minute pieces of glass on the kitchen floor.

Chapter 6

When Ellen discovered she could be pregnant, she made the conscious decision to do everything in the opposite direction to the one her own mother had taken. Mrs Phipps preferred 'to wait until the children are older, say, in their teens, then you can have a proper conversation with them'. But Ellen felt children deserved to be cherished: loved, taught, and secure in the knowledge their mother would always protect them and listen to them.

Three years and three months after the wedding had taken place, Ellen entered the hospital for the birth of her baby who was in no hurry to enter this world. Dr Peters had monitored them very closely and decided to induce the labour.

In the very early morning Father Thomas arrived at her bedside. He wanted to give her Holy Communion. She objected: she had been told it was 'nil by mouth'. He argued that did not count. He took one look at her and gave her the Last Rites (today it is known as the Sacrament of the Sick).

Ellen was later given an injection.

Both mother and baby objected so violently to the drug that the alarm was screaming in the hospital. The matron and the crash team arrived simultaneously.

'What's the emergency?' Ellen wanted to know.

'This,' said the matron, tapping Ellen's stomach. 'You are both allergic to the drug given to you for the inducement of labour. We'll have to use another one.'

Ellen was then prepared for the emergency caesarean operation. Both mother and child 'died' for a minute on the operating table during the procedure. The hospital did not have her rare blood group in their supplies so Mr Phipps rushed to the main centre to obtain the units necessary. In that ride he disregarded every red light on the roads to ensure he arrived in time to keep Ellen alive. All Ellen knew was she went onto the operating table as one person, but when she eventually regained consciousness, she did not feel as though she was the same person. Doctor Peters told her if she ever gave him a fright like that again he would kill her!

Afterwards Ellen was convinced that the Sacrament had saved her life and her baby's life as well.

Dr Peters had met Ellen's father when they attended the same school. It was at a wedding that Ellen met him. Ellen's mother being too ill to attend with her husband, required Ellen to go in her stead. The wedding reception was held at a nightclub that was completely booked out by the parents of the bride. Although only sixteen Ellen was allowed to enter those precincts as the event was private.

He was a sprightly, lean, and wiry man, with penetrating, curious eyes. As a medical student, he had rounded up a group of like-minded medical students. They purchased a building and proceeded to turn it into an accommodation for homeless men. These men were met at the door, sent into the showers, then given clean clothing and promptly given medical examinations. They were allowed to stay as long as they did not revert to their drinking and carousing. He was pleasantly surprised how many men changed the course of their lives as a result of the help they were given at a critical juncture. Of course, a number of them left, only to return time and time again.

Later Dr Peters learned the Chinese language and travelled to China to attend medical conferences on the herbs they used. He used to compare these herbs with the modern medical medicines that the West used to treat the same illnesses.

When they discussed philosophy and the manner of living, he told Ellen: 'If you follow the Ten Commandments properly, you'll never get sick.'

'How is that possible?'

'Simple. Take the one against anger, for instance. Anger can eventually have a devastating effect on your heart. People never consider the damage breaking these rules can cause internally.'

There had been no married life since Zack had learned that Dr Peters suggested starting a family as Ellen was already twenty seven years of age. Dr Peters had been adamant it would be dangerous to leave it too late: Ellen was five feet two inches in height and weighed eighty eight pounds. Zack was determined there would be no children: he did not know there was a child already on the way.

As her pregnancy progressed, Ellen trained to be a catechist and received her diploma at a special Mass celebrated on Candlemas night, a few months after Anne's birth She was convinced she would now have the knowledge to teach their religion properly to her child.

When Anne was seventeen days old, she was baptised on a Friday night. Father Thomas had disappeared into the ether, or so it seemed. From haunting their home, he was now never to be seen. Holding the well wrapped infant in her arms, Ellen tracked Father Thomas to the Baptismal font at one end of the church building. She wanted to know if he would be there for the celebration after the Sacrament. He wanted to know if he was invited.

'Of course, you're invited,' was the answer.

The evening started badly. Mrs Phipps was angry, though no one knew why. She had arrived very early with a massive bag containing everything she considered necessary to do the photographs as she wanted them. She grabbed Anne, put her on the sofa, and proceeded to undo anything that covered the baby's hands and feet.

'What are you doing?' Ellen wanted to know.

'This is to prove the baby is normal,' her mother replied, carrying on with her photographs.

'That's absolutely preposterous!'

'No. It's proof.'

Later everyone arrived after attending the Baptism in the church. One aunt was coy, another silent, just watching the show unfolding. Ellen's father in law was in a taunting mood, so Ellen kept as far away as she could; her emotions were very near to the surface after the trauma of the birth. Ellen's father tried to keep the alcohol flowing, and he needled everyone who approached him.

When Father Thomas eventually arrived, he grabbed Anne from Ellen's arms, and went to the round dining room table which was at one end of the room. He sat down cradling Anne while leaning his arms on the table. He later said that Anne kept him out of trouble.

After everyone had left, Ellen was left with the tremendous feeling that life had completely overwhelmed her.

Zack started working at the university. He left his salary cheque in the unlocked top drawer of his desk in his unlocked office. He enjoyed telling Ellen there could be no difficulty as everyone knew he would pay his bills. After more than a week of this game, he brought the cheque home and told Ellen to bank it. She asked him to approach the salaries department to pay his salary by bank transfer each month. Three months later he told Ellen his salary would in future be paid into his bank account.

It was only eighteen months later Dr Peters told her that Zack had been diagnosed as a 'schizophrenic psychopath with misogynistic tendencies', and that the child must never be left alone with him: he must be supervised by another adult at all times.

'That's a life without the possibility of parole!' Ellen cried, knowing that in South African law the father is the natural guardian of any child until the child reaches majority, usually at the age of twenty one. Cold with fright, she realised the most dangerous place in the world is right inside the family. What incident triggered this diagnosis is a mystery to today.

Ellen contacted Father Thomas to ask for his help as a psychopath is deemed to be unable to have the requisite consent to form a contract. The marriage was, therefore, a putative marriage, and any child born of it would be legitimate. He was sympathetic, but said she must learn to live with her situation. Now there was the daily terror she had to accept as a part of the rest of her life.

'How do you ensure that you never let something slip, however inadvertently?' Ellen asked Father Thomas.

'You keep anything else in your mind, and do not let yourself think about that subject,' he answered. This idea helped Ellen enormously as she was able to be sure she would never let the doctors' diagnosis slip when she spoke to anyone. She now routinely went to the child's bed whenever she woke at night, just to reassure herself that there was nothing wrong with Anne.

The next morning Ellen ordered two twin beds and the necessary linen to replace the marriage bed. She offered the large double bed to her mother or to her brother without ever revealing the real reasons behind her offer. Both those families entertained a lot, and either would be able to make use of the bed with its linen for guests. Mrs Phipps was incensed! At all costs, Ellen was to be forced to carry on as though she were in a normal marriage.

Ellen took Anne everywhere she went, shopping, parish visiting or to the various church services. She learnt the retired widows and families were particularly glad to see new life which brought back hope to them as well. Soon she was occupied with helping her local church with their books and parochial returns as well as the flower arrangements, while the child played happily with her toys on her navy, red and white woollen blanket on the floor.

Everything her mother did Anne copied. Ellen spent most of her time writing lists: Anne also drew pictures on pieces of paper. Zack decided Ellen needed to see a psychiatrist. He arranged a meeting between them. At the beginning of the first meeting Ellen was told she did not allow Anne any freedom, the child was always with her. Ellen was very surprised: Anne was only eighteen months old, where else was she supposed to be? At the end of the session, Ellen was handed a bottle of capsules, and told she needed them, and was to take them regularly. She was not informed about any side effects of the medication.

The next day she experienced such alarming symptoms that she refused to take another capsule, and she refused to see the psychiatrist again.

'You'll have to telephone him to cancel your next appointment,' Zack told her importantly.

Ellen refused: 'You made this appointment without giving me any information about it. You contact him.'

Zack telephoned the doctor immediately.

'She's refusing to take the medication.'

'She's a very sick woman. She cannot just stop taking her medication,' the doctor then went on: 'What did you say your name was?'

Ellen could not accept any diagnosis from someone who did not ensure who the patient was.

Anne began to lose her baby teeth. The next morning, she would find a tiny notelet from Miss Edwina Toothmouse who sent her a letter written in tiny writing. Anne was thrilled, she had not only received a coin but also a precious communication. Zack was furious: 'You're lying to the child!' Ellen was unable to reason with him. A child needed fairy stories: that was the way children learnt morality. He would not be convinced: he had never encountered any fairy tales. This row erupted with every tooth Anne lost, but the notelets kept arriving until she was old enough to realise her mother was writing the little tales for her.

Ellen decided to book Anne into a play school as there would be no siblings, and she must be able to interact normally with other children. Anne soon adapted to her new surroundings.

One Saturday Zack encouraged Anne to jump on a bed in a strange room. The child was so close to the bedside table that she cut her face so badly she needed medical intervention. The telephone call to Ellen was rushed, and told her not to worry Anne was on the operating table. When the receiver at the other end of the call was replaced, Ellen was frantic. She telephoned her father but her mother answered, and then said: 'We're not talking to you. You're not supposed to call us.'

'This is a possible tragedy. Please may I speak to Daddy?'

When she heard her father's voice, she asked him to help her track which hospital was treating Anne. He refused, and told her to wait for a telephone call. Ellen was devastated. Her family really had no kindness, and no sympathy. She waited until Anne arrived home with stitches on her face. She told Zack if another incident such as this ever happened again, she would inform the police that he must be charged with child abuse.

One morning Zack informed Ellen importantly that a famous client, who was referred to him by Father Thomas, was arriving at their flat to be given confidential legal information. It was so secret that he was obliged to lock her into her bedroom to ensure confidentiality. The door was locked, and only opened after the visitor had left the flat. Ellen was so enraged that she visited Father Thomas in his office. She asked him if he knew so little of Canon Law that it was necessary to play dangerous games. Why could the meeting not take place in a normal office? Zack was furious; Ellen was contemptuous: the whole world knew how intransigent the Roman Catholic religion was on certain points. In her view, the whole arrangement was ridiculous. There was no need for this interview to be conducted in her home, nor was there any reason to lock her into her bedroom. The client was unable to obtain the desired result.

On Zack's birthday Ellen had purchased a Devonshire cream cake which he claimed was his favourite. The afternoon wore on while she waited for him to arrive home. The door-bell rang. It was her father. He was in the vicinity, he said. She offered him a cup of tea. The door-bell rang again. This time it was Father Thomas. Both men eyed the cake appreciatively.

'How's the grave business?' Ellen's father started.

'How's the rip-off business?' Father Thomas replied.

'How about offering us a slice of that cake?' asked her father.

Then they tucked in, each trying to outdo the other. Ellen was at her wits' end.

'Can you leave some for Zack?' She asked weakly.

'There's plenty left over,' she was told when barely a quarter was left.

Zack was stunned when he saw his cake: a thin slice was all that was left for him.

Ellen continued to go to daily Mass and one day Father Thomas appealed for anyone with time on their hands to visit a fellow priest who had been flown to Johannesburg from a neighbouring country to have an operation.

At the hospital Ellen walked into the ward where Father Anthony was lying, his eyes already bandaged. In a few minutes she introduced herself then began to tell him about Anne's antics. He grinned, chuckled then laughed as the stories were related. This was the best medicine, he later told Ellen: at the moment she arrived and he heard her voice he had just realised what it would be like if he were left blind. It was an unthinkable idea as he used his eyes extensively for Church constitutional documents that were written in Latin, and had to be adjusted as the world and circumstances changed. Some of the orders were still regulated by medieval documents which could make modern living difficult. It was obvious he relished his work.

At his second visit to their home, Father Anthony asked Ellen if he could help her with what was wrong in her marriage. Terrified, Ellen knew that she was bound to this home until Anne reached her majority, or was very near to it. There was no other way to ensure Anne's safety. Ellen managed to smile and say: 'Please don't worry, Father, there's no sin involved.'

He never referred to this again. Nor did any other person. Over the years Father Anthony became a revered friend who visited their home each time he arrived in the country.

Chapter 7

Zack started looking for a house to purchase in the northern suburbs of Johannesburg where the average size of each property was about an eighth of an acre, or 350 square metres. The one he chose was substantially built with a surrounding brick wall in the front and a roll up door on the driveway. It was set so there was very little garden to manage. There were two roofs, corrugated iron which was covered by grey slate; and there were two ceilings, the traditional one and the meranti one left on display in the main living rooms. This meant the house was cool in the heat of summer but warm and cosy in the cold winter nights which could be as low as minus four degrees Celsius. The outside walls were painted in the palest yellow. Slate paving was on the pathway leading to the house and also on the four steps which led to a slate patio outside a picture window.

There was an entrance hall leading into a sunken lounge then into a dining room which in turn led into a large kitchen with an attached pantry. There was the main bedroom with its own bathroom, and three other rooms, two of which were used as studies, and a bedroom which could be used for Anne as well as a separate bathroom and a small cupboard-like room which Ellen had converted into a linen room with shelving that extended to the ceiling.

When Mrs Phipps first saw the house, she exclaimed that she wanted it! She ordered her husband to purchase it for themselves. He wanted to know what she would do with it: they already had a beautifully appointed home with special plaster on the ceilings. Did she want to sell their own home? No, she said, she wanted both of the homes! Zack quietly went ahead with his purchase. A long time later Ellen learnt that this house had been the Johannesburg headquarters of the Nazi sympathisers during World War II. Was this the reason Zack was determined to have this particular house?

The first night in the home Father Thomas arrived to bless the home, and to say a family Mass in the dining room where the fold-away meranti doors could be closed so that the event was not on public display. Ellen was astounded, she could not believe how lucky she was. She hoped this would make their home safer for the family.

No one mentioned the fact that there was no earth-leakage circuit breaker installed so that Ellen received a tremendous shock when she tried to turn on an electric light. Nor did they mention that all the water pipes would have to be replaced before anyone could live properly in the house. These major renovations were undertaken immediately with Ellen trying to cope with all the various contractors as well as for the city gas installations so that the gas stove would be able to be switched on by the relevant engineer. The final straw was the kitchen cupboard unit that lifted at the opposite end if anything was placed on it. She saw to the installation of new kitchen units as well.

When Zack purchased the house, he stopped setting any of his outside examinations and the marking that was involved because, he said, it was too much work. This meant Ellen had no access to any money at all. She had allowed Zack to be the second signatory on her bank account, but when his salary grew ever greater, he then wanted all their monies, including any belonging to Ellen to be in his account with Ellen as a second signatory. This meant Ellen was now completely dependent on Zack's goodwill. She suggested she now start working again as Anne was attending the local play school. Zack was furious: Ellen was to stay home. To fill her days, she started growing her own vegetables.

A family member was having a wedding. Four year old Anne was chosen to be a flower girl. When they were all dressed and ready to leave, Ellen noticed Zack seemed very agitated. She could not understand why. The first car arrived and Anne was put into the back seat. Anne had been ill, and Ellen was worried about a late evening for the child. Anne stretched out her arms to her mother. Ellen was placated with the suggestion that Anne would be fine. They were told Ellen would be collected later. Zack took Ellen with him and went into the house. He then locked Ellen into the house, and walked out to the car. She ran to the telephone to reach members of her own family to ask them to take her to the wedding. Each and every one refused her request. She realised the shocking truth of the words of her first employer: 'If you don't leave your family, and go far way, they will destroy you.'

When a fretful, tearful Anne arrived home very close to midnight, Ellen was rightly furious. She asked Zack if he wanted to be accused of kidnapping? She would be happy to lay the charge! Zack was very pleased he had achieved his objective, whatever that was. Afterwards, Ellen wondered what the significance of her absence from this wedding was? Of course, she was never given any photograph of the occasion. She always remembered this happening, as did Anne who now only looked to her mother for direction. She would always wait to see what Ellen would do.

This was exemplified when the time arrived for the Irish passport application forms to be signed. Zack had arranged an appointment with a lawyer who, he was sure, would bring pressure to bear on Ellen so she would sign the forms as Zack directed. He was relying on the principle of the blackmail of good manners. Zack, Ellen, and Anne were welcomed into the plush offices. The forms for Zack and Ellen were completed. Ellen was asked to sign permission for Anne to be included on Zack's form. She refused. For an hour and a half, they wrangled. Finally, Ellen said: 'When Jesus gave me a baby it was not to play pass the parcel with her! She either has her own passport or she is included on mine!' When it was evident Ellen would not agree, Anne's form was quickly completed and signed by all three family members.

When Anne was four Zack demanded that he spend time alone with her on Sunday evenings just before she went to sleep.

Once, Father Thomas suddenly said to Ellen: 'Get in there,' nodding his head at the doorway.

Ellen appeared by Anne's bed. Anne asked: 'Would you really go and leave me?'

'No. I'd have a big suitcase for you, with holes drilled into it so you can breathe. And I wouldn't even stop to take my handbag.'

The tears stopped, replaced by a wide grin. Anne was satisfied, she knew her mother never left her handbag behind.

But Ellen was furious at the gratuitous hurt caused to a little child.

One winter's night when winter was at its frostiest worst, Ellen decided to walk to her mother's flat in a high rise building where her parents had moved after selling their house. It was unthinkable to leave Anne behind in the house alone so they walked together in the dark when they judged Mrs Phipps would have arrived home from her work.

When she was asked for a small loan to last a few weeks, Mrs Phipps took her purse out of her handbag, and removed some notes. These she waved at Ellen who thought she would be given the money, however little it was. Mrs Phipps then pushed the notes back into her purse, and put the purse into her handbag, saying: 'It's so little, I'm sure you can cope without it. I can't drive you home because I haven't had my brandy yet.'

Without having been offered a cup of tea, the little girl and the distraught mother made their way back home in the now darker, icier roads.

'We're better off without her,' was Anne's brave reply.

The next day Ellen signed an agreement to work with a recruitment agency for short-term accountancy assignments. This meant that she would only have to wait two weeks to access her cash. Thereafter she would be paid weekly. She did not tell Zack what she had done. She let him discover it for himself when he arrived home before she did on the following evening.

To no one's surprise Zack was livid: 'I told you not to work! You must stay home!' Ellen did not know that this explosion was the result of the frustration Zack felt because Ellen was escaping his coercive control. She ignored every sulk, and tantrum, and tried to carry on with her life.

The sun was shining, the flowers were gently moving in the breeze. Zack decided to go the shop around the corner and to take Anne with him. Soon they arrived back, he was furious and Anne tearful. The beggars were sitting on the pavement enjoying the sunshine.

Zack offered them some money, in return they decided to compliment him on his beautiful child. He was suddenly enraged and refused to give the men anything to teach them a lesson.

'Did it occur to you they could have attacked you?' Ellen asked.

'No, I'm much bigger than they are. I can handle myself.'

Zack's 'fugues' were increasing. One Good Friday afternoon he was so terrifying that Ellen grabbed Anne and her handbag, and they left the house. Zack was sitting in the dining room, oblivious to their activity. There was no transport so they walked a distance of about five and a half miles to reach Father Thomas. When he saw them, he greeted them and then took them straight back to their home. His presence ensured that Zack would not be violent.

It was not long before another 'fugue' resulted in Ellen's door being broken by Zack's fist, before he turned to their bathroom door and broke it as well. Ellen never understood what induced these episodes, nor did she ever learn how to prevent them. She just ensured that she and Anne were never within Zack's reach.

One day Zack arrived home, his trousers and shoes were burnt. The pungent smell of smoke was overpowering.

'What happened to you?'

'I jumped on a fire to try to stamp it out.'

'Are you hurt?'

'Of course not, silly.'

'Where was this?'

'Outside the school.'

'Why didn't you pick up the sand on the pathway and throw that on the fire, or call someone?'

'I did not think of it.'

Zack never explained why he was outside the school at eleven in the morning. His clothes were ruined beyond repair.

When Zack received a demand to attend an interview at the office of the Receiver of Revenue, he refused to go: he sent Ellen in his stead. The official was astonished: 'You know you have no standing in this matter. We cannot discuss it with you.'

'Perhaps I can answer some of your questions,' Ellen offered.

'Who compiles his returns? Is it you?'

'Yes.'

'How have you survived living on the same amount for the last five years?'

'I grew my own vegetables, and made my own clothes.'

'That doesn't explain how his salary has remained at the same level for those years?'

'The minister,' Ellen named him, 'promised an increase over four years ago. This increase never materialised. That's why they call him "Blank promises"'.

'Yes, but this is really not good enough! He will have to come into our offices to answer all our questions! He should never have sent you in to do his dirty work for him!'

Ellen could feel the vibrant frustration that filled the poor man.

There was an occasion Ellen received a telephone call at her office. Zack was lying down on the floor in his office, sufficiently conscious to be able to refuse any medical help: doctor or ambulance. While she listened to what was said she was busy scribbling in her Filofax©.

'What were his symptoms?' Then after a pause Ellen said: 'I'll meet you at home as soon as I can get there,' packing everything into her large handbag, and pushing all her work related material into her cupboards and her desk. By this time one of her colleagues had run to tell her manager about the crisis. He arrived, keys in hand, ready to take Ellen home: he knew the bus would take her about two hours, whereas the car ride was only twenty minutes. The next day when Ellen spoke to their doctor and listed Zack's pain and all the symptoms she had been told, he said Zack had probably had a mild heart attack.

When he considered Ellen had settled in their new home, Father Thomas contacted the parish priest in Ellen's new parish to tell him that Ellen was a qualified catechist and suggested she help them with their catechetical programme. When she received the telephone call suggesting she should call at the presbytery Ellen was very surprised. She agreed. Soon she was teaching children who attended state schools on Saturday mornings. One week her lesson had taken her forty hours to prepare. She had looked up every reference possible, checked all her facts and was prepared to give what she hoped was the best lesson about the Mass that she could.

The rowdy class of pre-teens was silent, watchful, and fearful. Instead of launching into her lesson she asked the class what had happened. The answer was horrific.

'A boy in my class hanged himself on Thursday.'

Ellen then started her lesson as always. On the blackboard she drew a big circle, badly, always telling them they could draw better than she could. She then drew a cross from end to end, then made a square at the intersection of the cross.

Diagram of a Soul

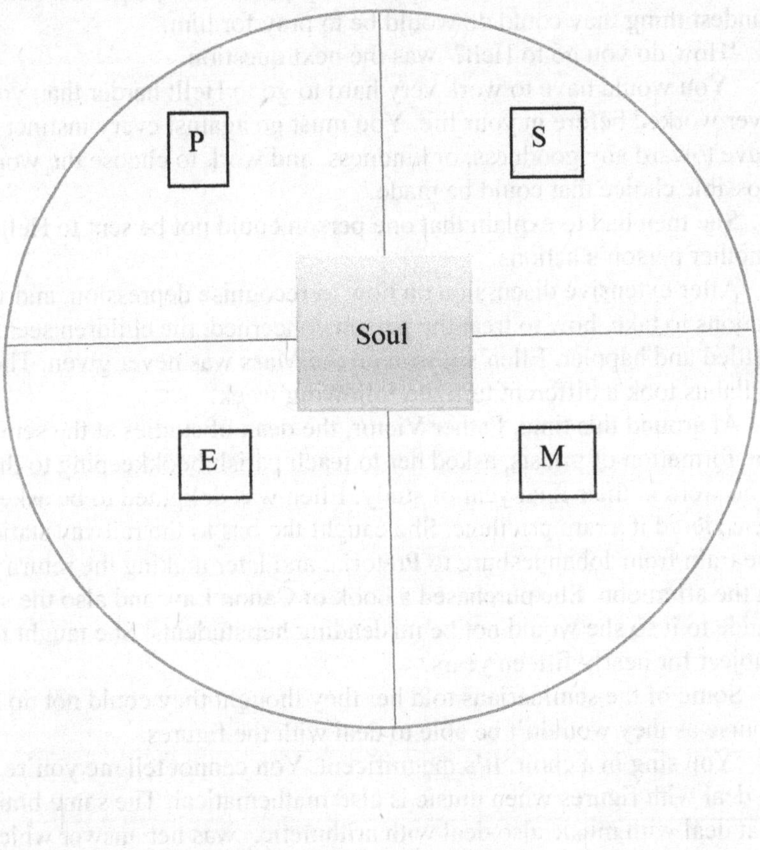

The circle was the whole person. She filled in each section, starting with S for 'spiritual', M for 'mind', E for 'emotions', P for 'physical, or body', and the box containing the 'Soul' was shown as interacting with every aspect of a person.

She explained how each person copes differently in any particular life situation. Only God was in a position to know all the different aspects concerning a person. No one knew what could be in anyone's mind at the point of death, so one could not be in any position to judge that person. The kindest thing they could do would be to pray for him.

'How do you go to Hell?' was the next question.

'You would have to work very hard to go to Hell: harder than you have ever worked before in your life. You must go against every instinct that you have toward any goodness, or kindness, and work to choose the worst possible choice that could be made.'

She then had to explain that one person could not be sent to Hell by another person's actions.

After extensive discussion on how to recognise depression, and what actions to take, how to treat the person concerned, the children seemed more settled and happier. Ellen's lesson on the Mass was never given. The syllabus took a different turn the following week.

At around this time, Father Victor, the dean of studies at the seminary for the formation of priests, asked her to teach parish bookkeeping to the men who were in their final year of study. Ellen was delighted to be asked: she considered it a rare privilege. She caught the bus to the railway station, then the train from Johannesburg to Pretoria, and later making the return journey in the afternoon. She purchased a book of Canon Law and also the study guide to it so she would not be misleading her students. She taught this subject for nearly fifteen years.

Some of the seminarians told her they thought they could not do her course as they wouldn't be able to deal with the figures.

'You sing in a choir. It's magnificent. You cannot tell me you're unable to deal with figures when music is also mathematical. The same brain cells that deal with music also deal with arithmetic,' was her answer which was greeted with a roar of laughter.

Then when someone else did not want to be part of her class, she asked: 'Can I come and work for you in your parish because you'll never be able to recognise any fraud?' This resulted in an even greater roar from the men.

Some years after she started these classes, she was walking down one of the main streets in the Johannesburg business district when a priest pulled her towards the building out of the way of the people thronging the street.

'You don't remember me, but you saved my life,' he said. 'Your classes helped me so much: I just wanted you to know.'

Later Zack decided Anne would no longer attend a state school: Ellen was expected to empty her savings account she was using to try to build up a pension fund for herself. Zack's pension was handsome – funded generously by his university employer. She started yet another unit trust scheme for her pension fund, which was also wiped out to fund the final year of Anne's education.

One day Zack decided to take Anne to see a film in a cinema in the central business district in an area where safety was a paramount issue. He told her to meet him outside the building: she waited for over an hour and a half before walking to the bus stop to catch the bus home. His answer: he decided to go elsewhere. Afterwards Ellen always took Anne to her cinema treats, including to thirty six films to help her in her French examinations. Ellen also began to learn how to speak French.

Chapter 8

The gas stove eventually stopped working altogether. Ellen bought an electric frying pan so she could prepare the family meals. Very soon she could see this was not a viable alternative. Zack had been very vocal about her spending. He refused to have the gas stove repaired or replaced.

Mrs Phipps arrived one Friday afternoon and wanted Ellen to accompany her to watch a special demonstration of the latest combination microwave and convection oven. Ellen agreed. They were shown how to use the machine and some of its attachments and implements. They were also allowed to taste the food that was prepared and cooked in front of them. Ellen was thrilled. This was the answer to her cooking difficulty. She purchased the machine and all the implements that day and had the various boxes packed into the boot and also on the back seat of her mother's car. Mrs Phipps was furious. She wanted to see the microwave oven and to think about buying it, but her daughter had acted immediately.

When Zack arrived home, he was livid: she had no right to undertake such a big purchase. Ellen said she thought she had solved the problem of how to cook their meals because he had refused to do anything about the stove.

Each Friday afternoon while Anne was at school, Ellen went with her mother to the course of lessons offered with the purchase of the oven. It did not take long for her competitive spirit to spark before Mrs Phipps also took the same model home.

At Christmas time Ellen decided to give Christmas cakes to the various couples in the extended family as a special gift. These cakes took an average of about two and a half hours each to prepare and cook. That year she made nineteen cakes and decided to give the final one to an aunt who was a favourite with her. When it was taken out of the oven and still steaming, Ellen was called to the telephone. She begged the two men to be careful around her cake. She returned to the kitchen to find Zack and Father Thomas were both eating from her special cake. She told them both: 'It's a miracle that you both aren't extinguished!' They just laughed. But Ellen never cooked another Christmas cake.

One Thursday Ellen lost consciousness as she tried to cross the road at a busy intersection. Lying in the middle of the road she heard someone say: 'Don't worry about her, she's probably drunk.'

The next day at her physician's office she was seen immediately, and given a full medical examination. When she was dressed and back in his office the doctor telephoned another surgeon in her presence, gave the pertinent details, and had her booked as the last appointment for the following day. After a thorough examination the surgeon suggested he would operate on the following Tuesday. Ellen was to be admitted to hospital on Monday.

When Ellen asked for more time to consider the consequences of the operation she was told bluntly: 'Do you want to designate the carer for your orphan daughter?'

On that Saturday and Sunday Ellen cooked thirty eight meals which were packed into the freezer because she knew Zack could not cook. When she arrived home after the surgery the meals could be heated in the oven. Ellen arranged for Anne and Zack to stay with her parents while she was in the hospital.

Ellen spent two weeks in the ward because Zack refused to have any help in the home for Ellen when she was discharged.

Zack had finally decided to take his sabbatical leave, and to spend the six months in England and Canada. He suggested he would leave his will with Ellen. He smiled at her, hoping she would agree. She did.

He then wrote, in longhand, a very detailed description of his wishes. He gave Ellen the widest possible powers from selling the house, which was in his name, to arranging to increase the mortgage bond, which was also in his name. The entire will was written in pencil, but he demanded that both the witnesses had to witness it correctly in black ink. At no time did he seek permission of the bank nor the university to this agreement. Once he was established in England, he telephoned Ellen and told her to go to the bank and to draw out around forty thousand pounds, and to bring the money to him in England. Astounded, Ellen refused. She knew the transfer of funds out of the country was subject to the most stringent examination. He was a lawyer, duly sworn to act as such, he would have known the will should have been written in black ink: Ellen wondered if he wanted her to be arrested for fraud? Was the will even enforceable?

In the meantime, Anne continued attending her school while Ellen went to work every day. Life was very pleasant, free from any arguments while Zack was overseas. They could even sleep at night as Zack was not there to keep them awake all night. From 16 December to about the middle of January each year businesses usually wound down; the building trade stopped for a well earned break. Ellen decided to take Anne to Cape Town over the Christmas Season. Anne's favourite opera star was the main attraction in a production at the opera house there. They were thrilled, and also decided to visit the wine tours. As Anne was so young, they decided to stay in the hotel each night. It was a highlight they remembered with immense pleasure for years.

In February on a Sunday morning, Ellen, Anne, and others went to the airport to collect Zack after his sabbatical leave had ended. Everyone was on edge, waiting to see him. When he arrived at his house that he shared with Ellen and Anne it took only forty five minutes for them to realise he was even more intransigent than before his break from the family. Ellen and Anne were both devastated.

As usual in South Africa the sun was shining merrily. Insects buzzed; flowers shared their various perfumes generously. It was a glorious day.

Zack, Ellen, and Anne were all home, sitting in the lounge. Zack was restlessly pacing around, while Anne was watching curiously, waiting for the day to begin to be shared. Ellen was suspicious. The telephone had been ringing, then Zack would pounce on the instrument, listen, and be short because the call was not the one for which he was waiting anxiously. Ellen had, as was usual for her, a pen in one hand, and a notebook in the other. This time the little book was being used to record all telephone calls to the home as well as every call outgoing to other people. So far, she had a total of forty nine calls with those names she could catch, and the morning was not yet finished. As the telephone was quiet, Ellen went quickly to it, and detached it from the electric plug in the wall. She then hugged the machine under one arm and walked away to the dining room.

'You can't do that!' Zack almost shouted.

'Why not? You can stay at the university and use your telephone in your office if you're going to live on it,' Ellen explained. 'Why are you running up our bill with your work issues?'

'It's important,' Zack huffed.

'So far, it's forty nine calls this morning that have taken up the whole of your time. If you don't want to spend time with us you might as well be at work. By the way, I'll be getting an itemised billing for all the secret calls today.'

'Oh, no, I'll prevent you from accessing that information,' Zack roared.

'Next time, don't blame me for the high cost of this bill: it's all your work calls.' Ellen then continued in a calmer voice, 'At least, it's quiet for the moment.'

Ellen had held the machine for just over half an hour. She pushed the plug into the electric socket and immediately it shrilled. Zack ran and grabbed the receiver: at long last it was the girl friend.

To her delight Ellen discovered the reprint of her favourite author on the mystics. These books had been unavailable for so long Ellen felt the drought. She purchased some of them, a few were in two volumes. She started reading them in the few minutes available to her, usually before going to sleep. Then she found that the second volume of the one she had finished had disappeared. She looked through her treasure trove to discover that so many were missing. When she asked Zack about them, she was told: 'I gave them to the convent. I told the nun I thought they might like to have these.'

'They weren't your books,' Ellen started. She was so ashamed of his behaviour but she knew he had applied what she had always called 'the blackmail of good manners'; he knew she would not dare to go to the convent to ask for the return of her books.

She resorted to hiding the books under her bed, but even those vanished. These books were not available for Ellen to purchase again. They had been a limited reprint. She felt she had lost a valued friend. She never found those books again.

Anne was been transferred to a college for the final year of her schooling. She did not spare herself in her studies, whether it was at a desk in her father's office at the university, or at her home.

Neither Ellen nor Anne was allowed any social activity except where the university events would reflect on Zack's reputation. He tried to prevent Anne from meeting the boy who was to take her to her matriculation dance. He wanted to go to the same place and sit at the next table to listen to them talking. Ellen told him not to be ridiculous: Anne was perfectly safe in a public restaurant. She did not know he was anxious about anything Anne might say about him. But Anne was excited and interested in the dance that was forthcoming, and the people involved. Now, Ellen began to experience the isolation that Zack had engineered around her and her daughter, while he was free to go wherever he wished to be.

He arranged for his colleagues to fetch him for work, and also for him to attend any functions particular to his field. Ellen and Anne were now struggling to get to work and school respectively because the bus system was becoming completely unreliable. There was no question of using a taxi: it simply did not arrive to take you to your destination. They were obliged to purchase a car and Ellen would be forced to learn to drive and obtain a driver's license. In the meantime, Ellen's manager owned a BMW car which was going to be made available to the post room staff if it were not bought by Zack. She wanted a small Mazda which would be inconspicuous. Zack was so determined to have a BMW that he agreed to pay the extra five thousand rand (about two hundred and twenty seven pounds sterling) to the retiring owner of the vehicle. Ellen started driving the car, continuing her lessons until she went for her driving test at the local grounds.

The official started to ask her how badly she wanted to pass the test. She replied either she was good enough to pass or she was not. This was not the answer he wanted. He wanted her to drive to her bank and to draw out an undisclosed sum. She refused, saying if she did not pass properly, she would never have the confidence to drive in the Johannesburg central business district. She failed the test. The head of the branch was leaning against the door jamb of his office with his arms folded across his chest. He looked at Ellen searchingly: she was trembling as she went to book her test for the following week. When she arrived again at the testing grounds the head official climbed into the car beside her and made her drive around.

He asked: 'Why did you fail?'

'Because I was not good enough,' she answered.

'Nonsense! You are! You've passed.'

Thrilled, Ellen replied: 'Thank you.'

Two weeks later the newspapers all screamed the headlines: *'Motor Vehicle Test Officials Take Bribes for Positive Results'*.

The big day dawned. Anne was being given a luncheon in her honour at the school awards ceremony held at the end of the academic year, just before the final examinations were started. She had won the awards, and also the floating trophy for the overall best student in the matriculation year. Ellen was told she could not have the day off (it was in October) as the year end was the end of December. She replied she would take it as unpaid leave. On hearing she was not to be allowed any day off at all, she replied: 'In that case, I'll not be at work on that day because it would be the utmost in ingratitude. My daughter has won awards, one being the floating trophy of the year, as well as having a luncheon being given in her honour, and she has been asked to give a talk to the audience; but I can't be bothered to attend! How ungrateful is that! She has achieved what no parent can ask. The least I can do is to be bothered to attend the function!' Ellen was graciously allowed to take that time off provided she had made all the necessary bank transfers to each branch of the company first.

At six thirty in the morning, she left work having completed all the jobs assigned to her for the day. She parked in the nearest parking garage, and sat in the car to read *Little Dorrit* until it was nearly time for the event to begin. She arrived very early, and took her allotted seat in the front row with other proud parents whose children were also receiving awards. The seat next to her was left for Zack, who only arrived as Anne was finishing her talk.

The luncheon was a minefield. Zack, mortified at not being the centre of attention, tried to humiliate Ellen in front of the teachers. He was amazed she had passed her car license examination only some days before. He had not seen her studying, and inferred it was not true. Ellen stopped him smartly: 'Your bus goes in the opposite direction to the one mine takes. You were not there.' It was the first time she had rebuked him in public.

'Let's go for a celebration,' Ellen suggested, looking at Anne's brilliant eyes.

'Oh, no,' Zack immediately objected. 'I couldn't possibly let my students down. Their first examination is tomorrow. I must be in my office for them.'

'Didn't you have time for them this morning?' Ellen wanted to know.

'That's not the same thing,' Zack argued.

Without further discussion Ellen drove Zack to his office, then took Anne to her celebration tea at the most prestigious Hyde Park tea room they knew. Over Earl Grey tea and lemon meringue slices they relived the joy of the day.

Ellen was working in the central business district in a building that overlooked the Library Gardens when Johannesburg was put into lockdown. In the Library Gardens there were wooden benches around the perimeter that were filled with loyal Zulus who were waiting for King Goodwill Zwelethini to arrive in state to address his followers. The day was sunny and bright, and the crowd was seated and absolutely silent without any movement. No one would have known these men were sitting there if they were not observed.

Standing near the window on an upper floor, Ellen with some of the staff who worked in the computer division were watching the crowd gathered below. One man was talking on his cell phone to a journalist of the major daily newspaper describing the events as they took place. Without warning a shot was fired from the top of the neighbouring building. The cell phone was immediately silenced. The crowd crouched, trying to avoid the hail of bullets while running away from the shooting that now erupted. Ellen witnessed some of the shooting that took place that day: innocent children and adults shot dead. It was in an area never acknowledged publicly.

All the telephone lines were blocked; the security guard was communicating with the police over a very loud black two way radio. One bullet penetrated the window of the office of one of the directors just before

Ellen entered the room. Fortunately, the man was sitting on the other side of his desk. Ellen never saw him sit there again.

The words running through her mind were: 'Anne, I want to see her.' The whole company seemed to be incapable of working normally. Everyone was informed the front doors were locked and no one would be allowed to enter or to leave the building.

Eventually the staff congregated in the entrance lobby. Ellen was in the front row. How she arrived there she did not know. She was worried about Anne. What would happen to her if Ellen were to be killed that day? None of this was apparent to those standing around. She was quiet and self-possessed as usual. She was wearing her grey raincoat with black trimmings and black accessories. She wore no jewellery except for her wedding and engagement rings, and the diamond on the engagement ring was pushed round into the palm of her hand inside her black leather gloves.

After the city was reopened, Ellen, with great trepidation, walked to the carpark and drove the car to the university to take Zack and Anne home. She urgently wanted to see her daughter, but Zack tried to force her to go home and to have a cup of tea. She was distraught, and threatened to call the police to find Anne as Zack just kept walking in and out of the library which only allowed access to students and staff of the university, and not to mere members of the public. Suddenly Zack discovered Anne in the library in her usual seat. Anne was pleased to be fetched so early; Ellen was not impressed with Zack's antics.

When Zack heard what was happening in the city, he pretended so well that he was going to try to 'rescue' Ellen. How he imagined he would be able to enter the city centre is a mystery. His pretence was such that he impressed those around him and they felt impelled to intervene, Ellen was later told.

The next day Ellen drove to work and parked her car in the parking garage which was situated very near to the old Johannesburg Stock Exchange. She turned with her back to the Exchange and walked along the street towards her office. As she passed the security guard, she greeted him as she did every morning and every evening. He grabbed her and pulled her behind the security roll up door to the garage and slammed down the door. 'They'll never find my body, now, especially after yesterday's slaughter' was her terrified thought. The place was suddenly lit with a brilliant blue-white light. Simultaneously Ellen saw a large group of people standing behind her. The guard told her: 'You arrive at the same time every morning, so we waited for you. We were warned some people are running down the street with knives to stab whoever they see.' The realisation that her life and those standing behind her had been saved by the man who always greeted her with a smile, and a comment was overwhelming. She was forty five minutes late for work that morning.

Ever after this event, Ellen was left with an overwhelming fear of crowds.

Two months later Ellen was asked to work in the seminary in Pretoria. Without hesitation she accepted the work and resigned from the multinational organisation in the central business district.

Ellen did not know the computer programme that she would now be expected to operate so she went into the local supermarket which was now expanding its market in the computer software division and purchased a copy of the software. The package included a complete manual of the programme as well as the report writing system that was now possible. After purchasing a computer, desk, and printer she spent a month learning everything about the programme. Then she purchased a spreadsheet programme and taught herself that package as well. Thrilled with her new abilities, she was now prepared for her new position.

Chapter 9

Zack was away from the home for such extended times that he did not know what Ellen was now doing.

The vice chancellor of the university invited Zack, Ellen, and Anne to certain social evenings which were attended by members of staff at the university, advocates, and their families. The monthly meetings were related to Charles Dickens, his writings, life and certain films or television series. It was not long before Ellen was asked to give a talk to start the proceedings. This was so well received that she was repeatedly asked to fill the breach, sometimes even without any preparation. Ellen was delighted. Various members also gave spirited talks which were always vigorously debated afterwards over tea and cakes. These were so successful that the vice chancellor started a Shakespeare edition of these evenings. There were also invitations to luncheons in the garden or in the large open room in his home. One night when Ellen and Anne were standing on their own, their host and hostess came up to them. He asked: 'Ellen, why do you persist in calling yourself a Phipson when Zack has that right?'

Ellen was astonished. The idea had never crossed her mind.

'Oh, that's not correct. My mother was Miss Phipson! How could he say such a thing? Don't take my word for it, check the records if you really want to know,' and she gave her mother's date and place of birth. She added that the town had had all its records burnt, but they had been recreated so the relevant information was still available if needed. The point being that Sydney Lovell Phipson, the writer of 'Phipson on Evidence', the English law reference book must have been included in his lineage. Ellen had never heard of him or his book before, and she had no knowledge who S L Phipson's descendants could be.

At another gathering she was asked about being pregnant at her wedding, Ellen's answer was simple:

'In that case I've made medical history. Assuming that I was already pregnant for three months at the date of the wedding in August 1972, and Anne was born in November 1975, that would mean I carried her for forty two months! Rather a long gestation, would you not say? A doctor could prove I was a primigravida!'

Ellen began to realise Zack was destroying her public reputation by lying. She decided to speak up at every confrontation that would occur in future. Zack, obviously, had no loyalty whatsoever to Ellen, and she wondered how long this had been happening. This was the reason that people were looking at her askance, ignoring her as though she were not there at the memorial dinners she was expected to attend. Sometimes she caught his colleagues looking at her as though they were eyeing a microscopic specimen. She was blunt in her responses now.

The Saturday began exactly as every one before had, with Zack leaving the house early. The afternoon was waning when Ellen was called to the telephone. A colleague working with Zack at the university wanted both Ellen and Anne to drive to the Market Theatre at one end of the central business district. They wanted to see a Zulu version of *Macbeth*. Then she heard Zack's voice: 'Don't you dare come here! If you do, I'll make sure you lose the use of the car. It won't be safe here.' His voice was cold, hard. Ellen knew this threat would be carried out: he would give the car back to the university, and they would have no transport. That night Ellen and Anne stayed home. It had never occurred to Ellen Zack wanted complete coercive control over both Ellen and Anne.

The years rolled on then suddenly Ellen's father was said to be very ill. Previously her father, at her mother's instigation, had telephoned her and told her: 'In future we will consider you dead to us, and no further contact will be maintained'. When her brother wanted to take her to see her father Ellen asked: 'Did he ask to see me?'

'Yes.' But this was untrue.

The family had work for Ellen: she was to see her father decently buried. There were difficulties, but they were now her problems. No one in the family would bear the blame for any of the consequences. However, she was aware of a great chasm between her and all the other members of the family.

She went to see the very ill man many times, after her day's work in Pretoria. She would stay with him and her now very subdued mother until it was time to fetch Zack and Anne from the University after Anne's lessons in Aikido.

Her father had been a fiercely proud man, independent to the last degree, but now he was uninterested in anything, and very docile.

The day was so lovely and bright that Ellen dressed carefully in a lilac three piece suit and started driving the car to the shopping mall. Without thinking twice, she made a U-turn in the road and turned the car to drive to see her father at his flat. She arrived then saw how shocking he looked, and telephoned his doctor who told her to take him immediately to the hospital. He would meet them there. For this service her mother never forgave her. It did not matter she would have taken at least two hours to travel from Randburg to Houghton to reach him, while Ellen was standing at his bedside.

When she received the call to have a priest administer the Last Rites she did not hesitate. She told the priest concerned her father had walked more than six miles from Hillbrow to Westpark Cemetery to pray the Rosary at his mother's grave for six months after she died. The priest agreed, and gave her father the peace of mind he needed by giving him all the Sacraments that were usual.

Once these formalities were accomplished her mother was hysterical: she had tried by every means possible to prevent such an event. She was almost prostrate at the thought she could not be buried beside her husband.

Ellen's father became unconscious, and was connected to the machines that were doing the functions of breathing and everything else in order to keep him alive. The doctor told her he would never be able to lead a normal life, and he would be tied to machines however long he lived. The last thing Ellen heard was how painful some of these processes were, and he was being given extremely heavy duty pain relievers. When she was asked, Ellen signed the papers agreeing to the hospital turning off all the machines. He died in the hospital the next day at noon, and his ashes were buried in the garden of remembrance of the Roman Catholic church in Rivonia. At his funeral, the officiating priest, who did not know her father, kept mentioning 'the body in the casket'. Ellen never forgave him for this lack of sensitivity. Zack projected the ultimate caring, concerned person, humble, sensible of the occasion. This was for public display only, never in private. He vanished. Someone called him: 'another Uriah Heep'.

For three days Zack did not return home. Then he arrived as though life was normal.

Six days after her father's death Zack suddenly said he wanted the three of them to purchase clothing. Once he reached the store, he took only an hour to collect the trousers, shirts, cardigans, and jackets that exactly totalled the limit of Ellen's account. He explained he had left his card at home so was unable to purchase those items on his own account. Ellen was appalled. Smiling, Zack asked the cashier to put the items onto 'his wife's budget account' which incurred interest at the rate of thirty per cent. Ellen demurred. The cashier did not listen to her, the account rose from nought to its limit, and the punishing factor was she would be paying this amount back over two years! Zack was euphoric. He could now impress people, and, most important, he would not have to pay for the clothing. He was also 'laying waste to Ellen's assets', as some people would describe this behaviour. The moment they all arrived back home, after laying his new clothes carefully on his bed, he took his card out of his pocket, and put it on his bedside table.

'But you said you'd left your card at home?'

'I forgot,' was his reply.

Ellen was astounded because she had consistently asked him to update his wardrobe, and he had just as consistently refused to do so. She was also panic stricken: never had she spent such an astonishing amount on anything in her life. She worried how she would be able to meet this commitment.

Chapter 10

Zack spent days away from the home. When Ellen asked, no one would say where he was. They assumed since she was a practising Roman Catholic she would accept any bad behaviour, and would be the usual complaisant wife. They would soon learn their error. It did not occur to any of those surrounding Zack that Ellen would consider being quiet and uncomplaining about his activities was simply one form of condoning, and being complicit in criminal behaviour.

It seems now it was widely known to everyone, except, of course, to Ellen and to Anne what Zack was doing. Then a lawyer died. Of the many stories she was told, Ellen never knew the truth. She only knew she was kept from any of the salient details. She could only pray for the poor man.

Ellen tried to continue with her life, driving Anne to the university for her studies every day then going further to her work in Pretoria. Some of her colleagues started making oblique remarks. She was unaware everyone was all agog to know the latest development. At least now they could sleep through the night with Zack absent from the home.

When he duly arrived, he was truculent, and aggressive before disappearing again. But not before their four little dogs rushed to attack Zack, jumping through the security door to the house. Immediately he ran to the second security door, and saved himself. The police captain told her those dogs knew she and Anne were at risk, and tried to save them. He said the fact the dogs were mixed breeds of terrier, Cavalier King Charles Spaniel, Fox Terrier, and Maltese Poodle, meant the threat to them was imminent and severe. The tiny dogs had not hesitated to try to protect the two women from the perceived threat.

One afternoon he was leaving the house but decided to turn back and told Ellen: 'You've often asked why I married you. It was only to have my university education funded.'

Anne's comment to Ellen was a devastated: 'If he took twenty seven years to admit why he married you, how can any woman trust a man again?'

Ellen contacted her brother's lawyer to ask if he knew of a good divorce lawyer. When he learnt she would be divorcing Zack, he offered to take her case. He then issued an ultimatum to Zack: stop staying away from the home for days on end. Zack decided to go permanently, leaving her with roughly the equivalent of fifty pence to run his house he was busy renovating. Ellen and Anne were living with the permanent dust, rubble, and upheaval while

Zack was living in comfort which he detailed at length. Now the contractors would no longer listen to Ellen concerning their work. They would only answer to Zack as they considered she had no capacity to be involved with the alterations. Zack, however, was not to be found.

The morning after Zack's departure Ellen visited a reputable jeweller and promptly sold her wedding and engagement rings for immediate cash for food and petrol. Zack now reinstated his outside examinations which brought him extra income. He also accepted the associateship with a famous firm of attorneys with a view to extending his work into mergers and acquisitions. This money also would not benefit Ellen and Anne.

Ellen was heartsore at leaving her work in Pretoria, but now she had to be gainfully employed to support herself and Anne, as well as to repay the bill for Zack's clothing. She was soon so occupied.

The afternoon Ellen's salary was available she and Anne arrived at the branch of Bearer Bank to draw cash to pay for food, and groceries. Her request was declined. She asked to speak to the manager. He told her that her access to any bank account had been withdrawn the previous day, the very day her salary had been deposited by her employer. She told him this was theft: no husband was entitled to access his wife's salary or wages under the Bertha Solomon Act (the Matrimonial Affairs Act). She also told him that her entire salary, without deduction, must be made available to her immediately or she would have no compunction in contacting the most notorious tabloid, and requesting this article be featured on their back page (familiarly known as the 'scandal page'). She gave him twenty four hours to contact the signatories on the account, whoever they were, and to have the money given over to her.

Ellen and Anne then visited the local branch of Dedbank where Ellen showed them details of her particulars, and they agreed to open an account in her name. Her salary was available to her the next day. Zack had an absolute horror of bad publicity, and he knew Ellen never threatened an action she was not prepared to carry out in full. It was a promise that could hurt him badly.

One of Ellen's lawyer's main interests was the subvention account that was held in Zack's name by the university. This fund was immediately deducted as a particular percentage of the gross salary. It was tax free, and was used, among others, to fund all the expenses relating to Zack's sabbatical leave overseas. Ellen ignored this fund. What she wanted was for Zack to refund the money she had spent on his education as he had reneged on his promise to let her read English at the university. He could pay this sum as a lump sum or pay it over a period of time. Zack then described this amount as 'alimony' on the deposit slips proving the receipt of the sum into the bank account. This meant that the authorities were immediately alerted and demanded a percentage of the sum as a tax. Ellen explained that this description was incorrect: it should have been called a repayment of a capital amount which had been loaned under certain conditions that were not fulfilled which meant the money was now due for repayment. The taxation authorities then allowed this amount to be free of tax.

When Mrs Phipps heard Zack had left Ellen and divorce proceedings were going ahead, she was frantic, and began to apply pressure on Ellen 'to stop her nonsense, and act like an adult'.

Ellen tried to reason with her mother: 'Life is intolerable with Zack. He doesn't allow us to eat and only lets us sleep for an hour and a half at night. His demands are absolutely unreasonable. If this continues, we will both be killed.'

'Don't be ridiculous! You're exaggerating!' Those were her mother's favourite phrases when speaking to Ellen. 'Marriage means you take the good with the bad.'

'Not when it means collaborating with, nor condoning another's sin.'

'There's never been a divorce in my family. I won't have it! You must stop your nonsense!'

As usual in any conversation with her mother, it was two people who could never reach each other, nor overcome the vast differences in their own value systems. Mrs Phipps never stopped trying to prevent the divorce, even to the extent of allowing another person to report everything back to Zack.

She could not accept the simple fact that Zack left Ellen; she was forced to divorce Zack in order to escape his domination, and to be allowed to have a roof over her head as well as to open bank accounts, and other accounts in order to continue to live. As long as the marriage persisted any bank official, particularly, would always defer to Zack because he was perceived to have powerful contacts, and they would be chary of upsetting him.

Zack was also openly pursuing other interests, and would allow neither Ellen nor Anne to participate in any public social events. These were important factors in Ellen's decision to go ahead with her divorce. The two final causes were an ultimatum Zack gave to Ellen, and that she was to consider herself subservient to his now acknowledged mistress. These are some of the reasons for Zack prolonging the process as long as he could to see if she would finally bend to his will. He ignored her Viking forbears. He could never understand any form of immorality, however popular in the modern world, would never be accepted by Ellen: she tried to live her life according to the Beatitudes, and the Ten Commandments, however short she fell when her actions were judged by these standards.

A few months later, after all his renovations to his house were finished, Zack had Ellen and Anne served with an eviction notice to leave the property. The three of them had lived in this house for twenty years. He intended selling the property, he said. Ellen told him and all the lawyers they had to give her adequate time to find accommodation. There were the four tiny dogs to consider. In a few weeks they found their home, albeit on a very busy main road. They took only their own possessions and left behind the bedroom furniture as these had been purchased with the proceeds of an inheritance Zack had received. This meant Ellen and Anne were starting their lives over.

The little dogs were happy in the very large back garden which they romped around.

After Zack had left the marital home, Anne was in the middle of her year-end examinations when he telephoned Ellen and told her he had cancer and he wanted to talk to heal the breach.

Shocked, Ellen agreed. But Anne had other ideas: 'Leave your bank cards, and cheque book at home,' was her very strong suggestion. Ellen did not argue, but emptied her handbag on her bed and put these important items away in a drawer.

She arrived at his university office. Zack opened the door to her, and without answering her civil greeting, said: 'Where is your cheque book, and your bank cards? Give them to me. The bank official said you must.'

'I thought we were going to talk...'

'First, give them to me.'

'I don't have them on me. Anne suggested I leave them all behind. Anyway, if I am to give these items to anyone it would be to the bank official at the bank's building. As my name is on these, I am responsible for them, so you are the last person who should have them.'

Zack was angry. Then he asked: 'Where's Anne? I thought she'd be with you.'

'She's studying. She said she didn't have time to waste on this nonsense. She told me she'd call the police if I'm not home by five o'clock.'

Zack looked at his watch, grabbed Ellen's arm, and frogmarched her to the car that she drove.

'Hurry up! You mustn't be late.'

When Ellen related these events to Father Victor, he told her she ran a risk because he had threatened to have her killed.

'But what if he really did have cancer, and wanted to atone? Surely that would have been shocking if I had not gone to see him?'

'What did he look like?'

'Exactly the same.'

'Then he doesn't have cancer.'

'He asked where Anne was, and when I told him she was waiting for me to arrive home at a particular time or she would be calling the police, he almost pushed me into the car.'

'So, he does believe what you say, after all,' was the quiet reply.

The telephone next to Ellen's bed rang at ten minutes past two one morning. It was Zack's colleague who was from overseas. He was concerned that he had been unable to contact Zack anywhere.

'We don't know his movements,' Ellen started.

'He must be there. Please let me talk to him,' the voice continued.

Ellen replied: 'Even the police are looking for him everywhere. They want to speak to him about a murder. He's said not to be at the university…'

The call was terminated abruptly.

The next evening Ellen received a telephone call from Zack.

'Don't use the "M" word.'

'Don't let your work colleagues keep on telephoning me at all hours of the night.'

Ellen never received another telephone call from any of Zack's colleagues.

A year after Ellen's lawyer had tried to serve the divorce papers on Zack, the sheriff's office admitted defeat: they had been unable to find him. This one fact impressed itself on Ellen's mind: it was the length that those around him were prepared to go to protect him. So, Ellen offered: 'Why not go to the tabloid?' She mentioned the most notorious scandal ridden newspaper. Suddenly, Zack arrived at the sheriff's office, signed acceptance of service of the papers, and further mentioned that he had been having an affair. He also named the other party. Usually, Ellen was told, the person just signed a name and date of signature when accepting service of any papers.

For roughly four years Zack kept Ellen busy with infinitesimal changes to the divorce agreement. This meant she spent hours checking each 'update', leaving her with insufficient time to sleep. After a day's work she had to check each 'change' that was made, even though previous errors were never corrected. She did not know about the personal tragedies that had erupted in her lawyer's life. She only saw he had not contacted her for over a year. He had not answered any email or telephone call she made to him.

One day she called at his offices to see his conference table was flooded with work from Zack's associateship firm so there was no time for her case to be resolved. Zack never intended to finalise it, but then discovered he would be party to a one hundred and eleven million rand payment that was tax free (roughly just over five million pounds sterling). To him it was unthinkable Ellen and Anne would benefit from this rainbow's pot of gold! He signed the agreement, with all the uncorrected errors in it, on a public holiday evening the night before the divorce court hearing would be held.

Without telling her he had signed the agreement, he telephoned her that night to try to persuade her she would be traumatised by the process, and she should not attend the Supreme Court hearing the next morning. His behaviour was most sympathetic and concerned. Ellen was suspicious. Any sympathetic behaviour had been dropped the minute the wedding service had been concluded. She kept replying she took her own responsibilities seriously, and would be present at the Court hearing the next day. He offered to have other people telephone her to describe how terrifying the process was. She reiterated her stance.

Her case was the first one on the roll.

The next morning the Judge granted the divorce decree the same day.

Zack was incommunicado that entire day. Ellen's lawyer desperately tried to contact him. She was never told why this was so urgent.

Only later did she discover that this was the third hearing, and the other two Court appearances were completely unattended. If this one was also unattended, she would probably be liable to be prosecuted and to be put into prison.

The following night Ellen received an email from Zack offering her one hundred and fifty thousand rand (roughly seven thousand pounds sterling) if she would agree to sign the form for an agreement of the annulment of the marriage in the Roman Catholic Church. She refused immediately.

She told Father Victor she had personal knowledge of two sworn affidavits in which he had lied, and of the steps she had taken in each case. She was not prepared to be a party to any legal process that would be abused. She and Anne had known for years of his knack of telling the most preposterous lies. They checked each story for external verification before they ever took any action.

Later, after the divorce was finalised Zack said he wanted them to be friends.

Ellen was incensed: 'You threatened to have us killed! That's a sick joke!'

'You'll have to be civilised enough to meet us in public,' he grinned.

'I'm not a hypocrite,' she spat.

After this conversation the police captain at the local police station told her: 'I don't have the manpower to keep you and your daughter safe. What nationality are you?'

'We have dual Irish and South African citizenship, with an Irish passport.'

'What are you waiting for? Get the hell out of this country!'

The last time Ellen saw Zack she was asked to drop off documents at his associateship offices which were near to her office. When she arrived, she was asked to wait until Zack appeared. She stood around the lobby noting there were no chairs for anyone to sit while they waited.

Zack arrived, preening. He was wearing a completely green outfit, suit, shirt, and tie; a colour Ellen always persuaded him not to purchase. The green heightened the colour of his face: pure puce. She wondered if his rages were the result of a heart condition. This could explain the very red complexion he usually had.

She merely greeted him and handed over the documents, then turned and walked away down the incline of the pathway. Her outfit that day happened to be the palest blue: she wondered if the mismatch of their outfits was important because they did not 'match' in any way at all as people.

Now that the divorce was finalised, and everything concluded, Ellen's bank and savings accounts had been almost completely eliminated. Then her lawyer decided to send her a final reckoning for her to settle. He knew she would be unable to do this so he suggested she transfer the car she drove to work to him. Immediately she realised this would mean she had no transport to her work. She requested that the account be 'taxed': that is, to be reviewed for any amount that could be diminished. The reduced account arrived very quickly. Without any other option, she sold the car to the same brand garage and requested the exact amount as that demanded by her lawyer. This saved her from paying any capital gains tax. Now she had no means of transport, and no ability to apply for any work opportunities.

At this time Anne's employment ended, along with that of a few thousand other employees. The bank had been a joint venture between two financial giants that decided to work with other partners in the future. Anne went into an employment recruitment office, and was granted an interview in London. She accepted the offer. Anne decided they were no longer going to be bullied and harassed. They would leave the country, and Ellen need not think she would stay behind: Anne refused to go without her.

Ellen then telephoned the Irish Embassy in Cape Town: 'What are the legal obligations we have to fulfil if we want to work in London?'

'What passport do you hold?'

'Irish.'

'Then just get off the plane and work.'

Ellen and Anne sold the house they had purchased a mere eight months previously, together with everything else they owned.

They were required to go for an exit interview with the senior representative of the Receiver of Revenue in Johannesburg. As they walked down the corridor, they heard a voice ring out: 'The professor's wife!'

He welcomed them into his office. He was a highly intelligent man who wasted no time on frivolities. He then started with the questions he wanted answered.

'Your husband has filed no returns for the last five years. Did you compile the returns for him when you were with him?'

'Yes, I did. I have no knowledge of his present situation.'

'I noticed that your returns were always filed in time. Don't worry about him, we'll get around to him presently.'

With that last word on her ex-husband's tax affairs, he swiftly helped them to complete the final forms which they signed. He gave Ellen and Anne each a cheque to finalise each taxpayer's file, then generously wished them well for their future.

After both cheques had been cleared, Ellen went with Anne to see the mortgage holder about the sale of their home they had purchased. The manager said: 'Most people just arrive, hand the keys to the house to us, and say that the sale of the property is our problem. You've been honourable, and have sold yours.'

'Anne is in finance, and we want everything to be finalised in the correct manner.'

The bank now wanted both of them to complete the final obligation statement before emigrating. This request Ellen refused. She wanted the form explained to them: she was not signing anything she did not fully understand. The officials were astonished: everyone just meekly signed the forms without reading them. An appointment was made. They went into a room where there were several officials present, all looking at Ellen as though she was a different type of specimen. They courteously took her through the process. First Ellen signed her agreement, then Anne signed the one she was given, after checking it was the same as the one her mother had signed. Ellen thanked the men, telling them her first law lecturer, an advocate, had told the class: 'Never sign anything you do not understand.'

Ellen's last current account was converted to an account which would be stringently monitored as any funds deposited therein would be immediately remitted to her bank in London. This was known as a 'Blocked Rand' account. All financial amounts had to be cleared through the Department of Inland Revenue before they could be transferred overseas. These transactions were carefully scrutinised, and only certain limits were allowed in each financial year which ended on the last day of February. Details of these accounts were held by the Receiver of Revenue.

Ellen and Anne had completed all the necessary legal and financial obligations which were necessary for them to emigrate. They both were convinced they would never see Johannesburg again.

Chapter 11

The airport was deserted when they arrived. They had extreme difficulty finding anyone to serve them a meal at any one of the outlets. When they went through the checking in process their luggage was accepted without weighing the bags as they were to be almost the only passengers on the flight: nobody wanted to fly as all the other bookings had been cancelled, they were told with a sad smile. The date was 10th October 2001, just a month after what was popularly called: '9/11'.

When their flight landed at Heathrow Airport, they went to live in a hostel. Anne had done her research, and decided a good place to look for employment would be close to the City of London. As they had never travelled anywhere overseas, it was as though they were transported to a mysterious fairy tale, though without any key to enable their understanding of it. The hostel was a place Anne felt sure Zack would never find. She was thrilled to be safe at long last.

For four mornings there was no breakfast, and the guests were muttering loudly. The receptionist asked Ellen if she was prepared to help out as she was always up and about early in the mornings. Ellen agreed. When she arrived in the kitchen, she started washing the sink out, as she had always done in her own home. The sink she had thought was an enamel brown, but it became lighter and lighter in colour as she cleaned it until it was a gleaming silver! She thought of this as an adventure while she waited for the recruitment companies to contact her with an offer of employment in her field.

Zack contacted Ellen by email, and told her gleefully he had found the bank official who dealt with her South African bank account, and the overseas transmissions, and had taken her to lunch to get details of Ellen's address in the United Kingdom.

Without hesitation, Ellen contacted the director of the South African Bank who dealt with the overseeing of international payments, and requested that he interview the woman who had agreed to a luncheon date with Zack. This was a potential serious dereliction of duty. He agreed to look into the matter.

Within twelve hours of receiving Zack's email, Ellen and Anne had moved to a different home address.

Eventually they both found employment and started what they were told was 'learning the London way' which was totally different from anything they had experienced before. Using distance learning, Anne started reading for her master's degree as she was continually told that her honours degree was insufficient for the work that was available in London. This was a two year degree so she deposited five thousand pounds sterling into a savings account, and instructed her bank that it was to be made available on the same date the following year. They did what she requested.

The following year when she tried to access this money to pay the university fees for her second year of tuition she was told:

'Sorry, we've rolled it over so you cannot access it.'

'But you rolled it over a month early,' Anne cried.

'There's nothing you can do about it,' said the Llanelli Bank official.

Distraught, Anne told Ellen: 'They've destroyed my degree! They've taken the money and invested it when I specifically told them I would want it at this time.'

Also happening then were a spate of letters in the various newspapers about the difficulties so many clients of various banks were experiencing in trying to change their accounts from one bank to another.

Ellen withdrew the money from her pension account and this allowed Anne to be able to carry on with her second year of study. Ellen also opened an account at another banking institution. Every night she would create the transactions that would be needed for the next month in the new account, then she systematically closed off those same transactions from Llanelli Bank until all her banking transactions would be routed through the new bank account. Llanelli Bank then had its credit card account, and savings account closed, with only two pounds left in the current account. Anne thought this was such a good idea that she also withdrew from Llanelli Bank, using the same actions that she had seen Ellen use.

They then arrived at their branch of the bank and requested the balances to be paid over to them in cash, and all accounts, including the credit cards, to be permanently closed.

It was a pity that Llanelli Bank did not know of Ellen's Norwegian Viking forbears: they would never have said: 'There's nothing you can do!'

Ellen's joy was overwhelming to learn Anne had passed her degree so well she was cleared for further study.

However, Anne was still told by recruitment agencies her degree was inadequate. She was seriously advised to read for her Doctorate in Philosophy. This dimmed Anne's pleasure in her achievement.

They continued in their separate careers, glad to be together, safe, and far enough away from all the previous trauma.

Seven years later on a snowy November day in London, the frantic telephone call reached Ellen. She had suddenly started crying while at a meeting at her office. Always she had been unable to cry prettily. Instead, her face and her eyes swelled and turned blotchy. It took hours for her face to resume its normal look. However, that day only tears were streaming down her face, but there was no swelling nor discoloration. When asked why she was crying she simply said she did not know. After some time, the tears stopped abruptly.

Ellen reached her home when the telephone was ringing. She told Anne she would answer the call then she would greet her properly. It was to tell her Zack had been stabbed to death: sixteen furious blows to his chest on a street in Cape Town. Ellen had started crying at the time of the attack, and had stopped at the time of Zack's death.

On Monday morning the manager took one look at Ellen's face and wanted to know what had happened. When she finished telling him, he could not understand why she still cared.

'One hopes for a reconciliation, however minor,' was her reply.

Zack's death was horrific. The students who formed a vocal force were very determined about the violence against a 'gentle' man: those who had known him for forty years and more said not one syllable about him in public. Was his sycophancy realised by those upon whom it was exercised?

There were many theories about the cause of this tragedy, but no proof. No one was ever convicted of his death. Just before he died, he seemed to be behaving like a tyrant: he was publicly issuing wild threats, instead of letting the due processes of the law run their courses. Later Ellen heard such a frenzied attack meant the attack was personal. Another mystery.

There is no doubt Zack was a very clever man. But, how many of all those who truly believed they understood Zack realised his mimicry of any emotion could be misread? Or that his mischievous tilting at authority could be malevolent, the serious results impacting badly on unsuspecting victims? Or that his coldness was endemic? He charmed, overwhelmed those subjects with his apparent interest then turned away absolutely once his interest waned, or his object had been fulfilled. Ellen knew he was not to be blamed for his lack of humanity; it was beyond his capabilities. This knowledge did not make her life, or her heartache, any easier to bear, especially in the brunt of the complete humiliations he felt entitled to parade in public. In return, Ellen could only turn to her prayer life.

As clever as he was, Zack never learnt the cardinal rule: no one is ever one hundred per cent wrong. He kept Ellen so busy, and deflected her so well, she never had the time to realise what was really happening. To a very large degree he achieved this goal.

In Zack's will he left his entire estate to Anne. There was no mention of his share of the one hundred and eleven million rand, tax free, a once only payment, nor what happened to it. Today there are still unanswered questions about this inheritance.

Inevitably, every lie Zack had told came back to haunt Ellen and also Anne. These lies were partially responsible for the impetus to tell this story. The truth carries its own conviction. Each heartache is carried to its finality in the peace that every person makes for himself or herself. Of course, most of the lies are never told to your face, only enjoyed in absentia. However, the consequences are felt when the job interview goes awry, or when people one knows just melt away. When things were at their worst it seemed that some people Ellen considered to be friends now used this time to extort money and to use emotional blackmail to achieve their dishonest ends. It was proved to be true, what Father Victor had told her: 'This is something you will never escape. You will never be free of it.' How shockingly apt.

We concentrate on everything that went wrong, but we forget all those things that went right. It is then one's habits, and hobbies are important. Robert Browning's *The Ring and the Book* was such a delight to Ellen. She marvelled at the poet's understanding of human nature that enabled him to envisage so perfectly the emotions of everyone caught up in that tragedy. His observations were proved to be correct when documents were discovered in an Italian library, was it one hundred and sixty eight years later?

Reading, as always, saved Ellen. Years later Ellen discovered the books that helped her to understand something of what her life had been; something of what had made Zack into the street angel and house devil he became. She wondered if her life had been saved by her divorce, and also the extreme physical distance from the man he eventually became.

The final thought about Zack was that neither Ellen nor Anne had one pleasant memory of the person they had known. What an indictment!

Chapter 12

Eleven years after the death of Mrs Phipps Ellen was taunted about her mother's burial place. When she was told Mrs Phipps was buried in the same garden of remembrance of the Roman Catholic Church where her father had been interred, Ellen cried: 'How was this possible when she was a non-practising Methodist who hated the Roman Catholic Church with a virulent passion?'

Ellen promptly emailed the attorney who had dealt with her late mother's estate. He replied, telling her to contact the relevant church directly, as this was out of his province. She then emailed the secretary at the presbytery. To her horror she learnt that her mother was given the cover story that belonged to her, Ellen: the twenty three years of working for the Roman Catholic Church; as a catechist, and so on. Various people now told her of the great love her mother had had for the Church! Ellen recognised this for the lie that it was. Not one of those she had contacted would accept her refutations of their concepts. Mrs Phipps was given a full Roman Catholic burial, despite her lifelong hatred of Roman Catholicism, which bordered on the pathological, and never having been received into the Church! Mrs Phipps had had no intention of ever being separated from her husband, even in death. What price family honour now…

Ellen was devastated. The shock of this abuse of the Sacraments horrified her absolutely. But life goes on, regardless of emotions. As many women before her, and many will later, Ellen learnt to carry on with the seemingly frivolous demands of her time. Three things enabled Ellen to cope: her faith, her books, and a teaspoon of hope.

Acknowledgements

My thanks go to Mrs Stella Temple, the late Father Bonaventure Hinwood, O.F.M., the late Mr Lionel Hinwood, the late Mrs Clara (Claire) Hinwood, Mrs Catherine (Cathy) Wilkinson, Mr Kazim Wurmezyar and his family, all of whom were kindness personified in the tragedy that followed.

My thanks go to Mary Turner Thomson, whose book helped to inspire me to tell this story. She gave me some valuable hints about the writing process. My thanks go to Jessica Bell Design who created the stunning book covers. My thanks go to Polgarus Studio for their brilliant work on the formatting of the e-book.

The various drafts have been checked by a witness who was present at virtually every step of this journey, and who also shared much of the terror that was present. There are many other similar incidents that may be shared one day. This witness has been unfailingly generous in time, support, and kindness, all of which can never be repaid.

For those who are legally inclined there are documents and court files which can be used to verify these facts. As this account was written during the coronavirus pandemic (COVID-19) crisis I have made no attempt to consult any documents held in safe keeping.

As I have no medical or psychological training, I have given no such judgement, nor do I give an opinion on the man's state of mind. The medical opinions quoted were those of medically qualified personnel. All I have done is to try to state as accurately as I can some of the events which unfolded, and some of the results which I believe to reveal his possible perspectives.

Any error is mine alone.

Books that have helped in this envisioning of these events:

Paul Babiak, Ph.D. & Robert D. Hare, Ph.D., *Snakes in Suits: When Psychopaths Go to Work* (HarperCollins, New York 2007)

Malcolm Gladwell, *Blink* (Penguin Books, 2006)

Malcolm Gladwell, *David & Goliath* (Penguin Books, 2013)

Robert D. Hare, PhD, *Without Conscience: The Disturbing World of Psychopaths Among Us* (The Guilford Press, 1993)

J. Reid Meloy, *The Psychopathic Mind: Origins, Dynamics, and Treatment* (A Jason Aronson Book, Rowman & Littlefield Publishers, Inc., 2002)

Mary Turner Thomson, *The Psychopath: A True Story* (Little A, Seattle, 2021)

CPSIA information can be obtained
at www.ICGtesting.com
Printed in the USA
LVHW101908280122
709673LV00008B/759

9 781739 850524